Advance Praise for *Wild Moments*

This book ignites the magic of animal encounters in the wild woolly North. Read it and be transported.

—Bernd Heinrich, author of *The Snoring Bird* and *Mind of the Raven*

The soul of the North lives in its creatures, and *Wild Moments* distills those heart-stopping moments when their lives and ours intersect. Whether it's an encounter with an angry grizzly or an indomitable wolverine, a boy's first salmon or the last musk ox of a dying herd, these stories—written by some of the best North Country writers of natural history—are a glimpse at the fierce, vital heart of the continent's roof.

—Scott Weidensaul, author of *Return to Wild America* and *Of a Feather*

The delightful essays assembled by Michael Engelhard in *Wild Moments* make the creatures of the North accessible to everyone, even to those who will never see them firsthand. These stories remind us of what is at stake as wild landscapes shrink and the climate changes, and of our responsibility to take up the causes of animals that are dependent on the frozen back-of-beyond.

—Stan Senner, Audubon Alaska

Wild Moments is a window into animal encounters and the thoughtful humans relaying those. This book provides enlightening visits with animals and people, far-flung across the country of caribou and bear, snow geese and ground squirrels, salmon and whales. All without even having to shovel out your own door.

—Seth Kantner, author of *Ordinary Wolves* and *Shopping for Porcupine*

The stories collected in *Wild Moments* vividly evoke the compelling landscape of the far North. They remind us of the ecological and cultural importance of a place where survival depends on cooperation between humans, on animals, and on respect for the forces of nature—and why what happens in this exquisitely sensitive part of the world ultimately matters to all of us.

—Elizabeth Grossman, author of *Watershed* and coeditor of *Shadow Cat*

Wild Moments is not so much a collection of stories about encounters with wild animals as it is an account of the love affair that blooms when animals allow us into the space where their world overlaps our own. And like any good love affair, it is not so much a single event as it is a compendium of moments that span a full continent of experiences and emotions. Wonder and elation abound in Karsten Heuer's *Calving*; Hank Lentfer's account of cranes in migration is a pitch-perfect tale of subdued affection; in *Porcupine Wars*, Debra McKinney charts the almost-parental transformation of irritation into love through the deft alchemy of humor. And lest we disregard the Gothic side of love, there is the heartbreak of Steve Kahn's *Heart Underfoot* and the murderous dysfunction of Daniel Henry's crows. These and more than two dozen other stories by some of the best writers in the Northwest provide a heady tale of love that is worthy of space on any wildlife lover's shelf.

—Lynn Schooler, author of *The Blue Bear*

Wild Moments is the next best thing to being there. The poignant stories flowing from our interaction with these "other nations" are reminders that America's last wildlife haven is at risk of being lost to the juggernaut of development. That is, unless we decide together that endless wild moments are worth more than quick fixes to long-term problems.

—John Toppenberg, Alaska Wildlife Alliance

WILD MOMENTS

Also by Michael Engelhard

Where the Rain Children Sleep
Hell's Half Mile
Unbridled
Redrock Almanac

WILD MOMENTS

Adventures with Animals of the North

Edited by Michael Engelhard

University of Alaska Press
Fairbanks

© 2009 University of Alaska Press
University of Alaska Press
PO Box 756240
Fairbanks, AK 99775-6240

The publication was printed on paper that meets the minimum requirements
for ANSI/NISO Z39.48–1992 (R2002).

Printed in the United States on recycled paper.

The Library of Congress has cataloged the paperback edition as follows:

Engelhard, Michael, 1959–
Wild moments : adventures with animals of the north / edited by Michael Engelhard.
p. cm.
Includes bibliographical references and index.
ISBN 978-1-60223-048-4 (pbk. : alk. paper)
1. Animals—North America—Anecdotes.
2. Animals—Arctic regions—Anecdotes. I. Engelhard, Michael, 1959-
QL151.W56 2008
591.97--dc22
[B]
        2008050768

Interior and Cover Design by Melissa Guy
Cover Images by Patrick Endres
Illustrations by Nancy Behnken

We need another and a wiser and perhaps a more mystical concept of animals. Remote from universal nature, and living by complicated artifice, man in civilization surveys the creature through the glass of his knowledge and sees thereby a feather magnified and the whole image in distortion. We patronize them for their incompleteness, for their tragic fate of having taken form so far below ourselves. And therein we err, and greatly err. For the animal shall not be measured by man. In a world older and more complete than ours they move finished and complete, gifted with extensions of the senses we have lost or never attained, living by voices we shall never hear. They are not brethren, they are not underlings; they are other nations caught with ourselves in the net of life and time, fellow prisoners of the splendour and travail of the earth.

—Henry Beston, *The Outermost House*

* * * *

Art can never replace, certainly not explain that adventure among the Others which remains central to our lives, though it is the principle means of evoking it.

—Paul Shepard, *The Others*

List of Illustrations

Contents

FEATHERS

Acknowledgments

No writer works in a vacuum. This becomes never more obvious than with an anthology. I would like to thank the following people who made this project their own: Robert Mandel, for seeing the need for books about the North that speak with many voices; Elisabeth Dabney, for finding the means and for guiding this one to its completion; Irene Trantham and Rachel Fudge, for help with grooming the prose; all contributing writers, for their trust, commitment, and patience; all writers who shared stories that, for one reason or another, did not end up between these covers; Wayne Grady, Sherry Simpson, Anne Coray, and Marybeth Holleman, for widening the circle of wordsmiths enthralled by other than urban bipedal life-forms; Fran Mauer, for insights into musk ox history and biology; Jo-Ann Mapson, for bringing the Henry Beston quote to my attention; Patrick Endres, for a photo worth a thousand words that gives me goose bumps every time I look at it; Nancy Behnken, for her skillful renderings of northern wildlife, and Hank Lentfer, for pointing me toward them; Margaret Craft, for involving me in a failed raven rescue, which sparked the idea for this collection; and, ultimately, Melissa Guy, for another expertly designed book and for facing not only bears, but also everyday life with me—which can be just as daunting.

May you all find moments of wildness when you need to.

Introduction

A few years ago I was guiding a backpacking trip in Alaska's Brooks Range, an Arctic extension of the continent's spine. One scene from that trek burned itself into my memory; unrivaled by other backcountry episodes, it keeps quickening like an ember when it is stirred. In less time than it takes to lace up my hiking boots, notions of invulnerability had turned to ashes. I was *not*, after all, exempt from Nature's accounting.

During a layover in upper Joe Creek we struck out to bag one of the unnamed peaks that crowd the valley, or rather, to succumb to the view from the top, of range upon range marching toward the horizon. While we were crunching through gravel past hedgerows of willow, I chatted with the group strung out in the wash. Near a brace of limestone bluffs, belligerent coughing interrupted our footsteps and conversation. *Bull caribou*, I thought, as I scanned the slopes for movement.

For days we had tracked caribou along the ruts they braid into marshland, over passes, down broken defiles, fording streams fat with boulders, waist-deep in snowmelt or up to our kneecaps in mop-headed tundra, trying to get within optimal camera range, which meant close enough to hear the herd's voice—its grunts, groans, and snorts a parody of arthritic men—or, closer still, what sounded like knuckle cracking: the tendons in feet that plied aufeis[1] and scree and post-holed the boggy pits between tussocks with the efficiency of pistons. In the migration's wake we had stalked wildness. Next thing we knew, it came barreling down at us from a ridge—huffing, jaws snapping, ears flattened.

"Cub and two sows," I called out to my clients. My mind somersaulted, scrambling language. A female grizzly, a blond bulge of muscle and fur, rippled downhill with twin teddy bears in tow.

Following my lead, the group scuttled up the embankment, determined not to panic or turn their backs to the bear. We then stood and faced carnivorous disenchantment. As I fumbled with the pepper spray's safety, I understood hermit crabs caught outside of their shells. Every fiber in my body itched to run, or at least to curl into fetal position before impact.

1

The sow reached the creek bed sixty feet from us.

To everybody's surprise, a lingering trace of our scent stalled her like an electric fence. In one fluid motion she pivoted, reprimanded one of the fuzz balls at her heels with a plate-size paw, and blustered up the wash, her cubs trailing as if attached by rubber bands.

Dumbfounded, we tried to coax our heart rates back to normal. The tundra was awash with adrenaline, abuzz with color and detail. The air seemed sweeter, the sun warmer. We flopped down and decompressed, our voices overlapping in disbelief.

Any attempt to fit the scuffle into a quotidian frame of reference failed. We had teetered at the brink. We had passed through moments in which nerves and ligaments could have snapped, trajectories could have changed.

After fifteen minutes—long enough for the sow to traverse several ridges and valleys if she chose to—we continued our hike. Each rock-bear on the hillside appeared ready to trundle. Around the next bend I promptly spotted her again. She was contouring a slope high above. But no, that one looked different. Its legs were the color of freshly cut peat, darker than the body; its size and shoulder hump declared it a male. The boar paid us no attention. He ambled through talus to a razorback ridge, where debris from the mountain swallowed him.

Craving a plot for apparent randomness, we replayed both sightings in search of clues.

Most likely, the sow had first scrapped with the boar. (Male grizzlies kill offspring by rivals to better the chances of their own genes.) She must have been riled up already when she heard us in the wash. Poor-sighted like all bears, she then rushed at the new trespassers to protect her cubs. As soon as she realized her mistake she bolted in terror, as most grizzlies will upon getting a whiff of people.

By fitting the pieces together, we made sense of the experience. We would revisit it for years to come—embellished, refined, acted out, or on paper—whenever bear behavior cropped up as a topic. In the retelling we construed meaning, and the emphasis slowly shifted from personal, localized lore to link with larger mythologies.

According to anthropologists, brushes with cave bears or communal mammoth hunts provided the raw stuff for some of our earliest stories, the means by which we condensed and transferred knowledge crucial to our survival. At the same time, these accounts marked common ground beyond the human realm. They helped us cross boundaries. They yielded symbols of potency, figures of speech, models of kinship with the natural world. They rendered existence sublime, vesting it with more than the nuts-and-bolts business of staying alive. Early Europeans emblazoned walls at Lascaux, Altamira, and Chauvet with murals animated by grease-fed, sputtering stone lamps. Under the pale fingers of spotlights, their creations are stirring again (sometimes as unfinished outlines beckoning our imagination): bears lip the ground for a taste of spring, adjacent to reindeer, aurochs, wisent, and rhinos that flaunt bulk or weaponry at dangers yet to materialize; less defensively gifted but comforted by the jostling of multitudes, horses with absurdly delicate feet and bellies taut as drumheads perk up, swivel stub ears, flare nostrils, and flex haunches—primed to dodge tawny-limbed lions, or leopards about to uncoil into vortices of muscled panic; on another panel, signifying transition perhaps, an antlered man-stag bends at the waist as if still only practicing upright posture. By infusing cave paintings and visions as much as they did words, Pleistocene beasts gave us art. Linguists suggest that language itself began as squeaks, warbles, and bellows when our ancestors mouthed birdsong or hyena laughter to attract prey or slip into altered realities. Animals therefore not only accelerated our physical evolution but also made us *sapiens* in a fuller, cultural sense.

With the majority of North Americans now living in designed environments, we need wild animals and their stories more than ever. We need them to remember that beneath the veneer of our language, our civilization, something feral still purrs. We need them because—our shared pasts notwithstanding—they don't remind us of us.

Whether in urban or wilderness settings, run-ins with animals rupture our daily routines. They trigger awe as easily as they do sweaty palms. They incite curiosity or compassion, rousing us from self-centeredness. They delight or dismay but hardly ever leave us unmoved. Not unlike us and sometimes within sight of our doorsteps or tents, denizens of the wilds court, mate, give birth, raise their young, fight, play, build, forage, kill, suffer, and die. Forever mysterious, they cast subtle spells. They rarefy the present, prompt lasting memories, reveal our true natures, or at best, transform us. We cherish these chance meetings and fashion them into stories that acknowledge fundamentals: Our heritage. Our connections. Our responsibilities.

Surpassing the continent's heartlands, its northern margins present unrivaled opportunities to come face to face with these "others," especially with charismatic creatures like bears, whales, and eagles, which by now are rare or extinct throughout much of their original range. But the North's tundra, its mountains and frayed coastlines, its boreal and temperate rainforests sustain more than just a few iconic species. Expanses that might strike some people as barren twitch with seasonal activity. Ptarmigans scuff angel wing marks into the snow. Voles tunnel through muskeg, while fox kits practice pouncing on them. Skeins of geese striate the sky—honking to keep from unraveling—and on cliff ledges, peregrines strive to raise chicks before frost urges their departure south. Ignoring the borders of countries or states, migrants like salmon, caribou, and cranes are the land's connective tissue, reminders of geographic as well as biological realities. Sadly, development and a climate crisis now curtail life in America's last best places.

When I approached a known poet about this project, he seemed unconvinced of the need for such a book. "You know how it is with moose," he said. "Seen one of 'em, seen 'em all." It took me an instant to decide he was probably teasing. Reflecting on our conversation afterwards, I thought he wanted me to dig deeper. Who, really, could claim to have seen moose in all of their moods, the full repertoire of gangly grace? Most wildlife encounters are fleeting affairs. Bird-watchers often fail to ID their prize. Fishermen unhook their catch as its rainbow starts to fade. Even hunters finish the chase quickly, with a burst that can equal epiphany. Field biologists, on the other hand, may gain long-term perspectives but too often narrow their focus, dismiss "anecdotal evidence," and bury much of life under data.

The writers in this collection have "seen" animals the way poets do. They've distilled an essence—the magic and unpredictability, the humor, the pathos, the bone and gristle, the smell of blood and the softness of fur. Beyond animal nature, they offer glimpses of our own, thrown into relief by contact with fellow beings. In their stories the personal frequently intersects the political, as, inevitably, joy mixes with grief. Smart, witty, wise, perplexed or enchanted, but always engaged, their voices join in a chorus as polyglot as the menagerie they describe.

Although these essays are rooted in landscapes known intimately by only a few people, each one touches upon universal themes—the desires and dilemmas, concerns and choices that spring from our tangling with the untamed. While not all of them address threats to the environment, each one clearly shows what is at risk of being lost.

As I type these words, news headlines inform us that, *irreversibly*, by 2050 two-thirds of the world's polar bears, including every last specimen in the United States, will have perished as a result of melting sea ice. Put differently, cubs emerging this spring from dens along the Beaufort Sea will be the last generation of Alaska polar bears. Other populations are likely to follow in similar declines or have already preceded the white bear's, like the belugas of Cook Inlet, North Slope musk oxen, and Aleutian sea otters. Before long, wildlife and people in more moderate latitudes will be affected.

As indicators for a healthy planet, northern animals inhabit refuges of hope. Though we may never cross paths with a wolverine, startle a griz at some fishing hole, or stand transfixed as loons ululate their evensong, it is good to know they are out there, that the potential for authentic adventure, for surprise and freedom, persists.

PRESCRIPT

(Prescript: announcement; imperative; notification; responsibility; summons; ultimatum. —Roget's Thesaurus)

Signs from the Edge of Life

DANIEL GLICK

I'd been in carnivore country before. In Yellowstone's Hayden Valley, my horse spooked at the sight of an upright grizzly, and I nearly slipped a stirrup and joined the food chain as an edible link. It was a singular feeling, the hair-prickling tingle of being prey.

The first time I went to Alaska's North Slope, it was on the heels of another tromp through grizzly country—in Montana. I'd strapped on a backpack and a can of bear repellent to join United States Geological Survey researchers as they measured how fast Glacier National Park's storied ice flows were melting. On that trip we saw no bears, although a mountain goat nearly decided to butt heads with me when he interrupted my middle-of-the-night pee.

I was feeling a little expansive when I found myself in Barrow and wanted to go for a stroll near Point Barrow to get a feel for my new surroundings. Kenneth Toovak, an Inupiaq elder and former whaling captain, warned against it. Some polar bears had ridden in on broken-up sea ice and come to shore recently, and the ice blew away without the bears on it. There were a bunch of them near town.

I inquired if perhaps I should just take some bear spray along.

He laughed, a full-throated, head-tilting guffaw. "Well," he said, "that way you could spray yourself in the face, so you wouldn't see anything while he ate you."

I didn't take the walk.

A few years later, I returned to the Slope to research the effects of climate change on the Arctic and ran into my first polar bear in the company of photographer Steven Kazlowski. In a frozen lagoon with a little swimming hole cut in the middle, a four-year-old sow tossed about what appeared to be a plastic toy. Looking through Kazlowski's telephoto lens, the unusual plaything came into focus: the "toy" was a walrus flipper. The white-fleeced sow twirled the flipper in her teeth, hurled it ten feet in the air, and watched it land in the hole in the ice. She then dove headlong to retrieve the flipper, leaving only the bottoms of her furry hind paws pointed at the blue Arctic sky. Surfacing, she heaved her 350-pound frame back onto the ice edge with a jaw-dropping display of strength, then shook her darkened, water-slicked fur until she was fluffy and white again. As the light edged toward perfect, she lobbed the flipper some more, jumped in the water, and repeated the moves over and over. A second sow rambled up, and the pair growled and wrestled together before wandering out of sight. The curious behavior had no possible explanation besides what it appeared to be: a well-fed polar bear playing on an autumn afternoon as if she didn't have a care in the world.

Unfortunately, this lighthearted scene showcasing the polar bear's remarkable fit to its icy habitat belies the problems faced by *Ursus maritimus*, a species headed for an uncertain future in a rapidly changing circumpolar world. From chemical pollution to oil drilling, hunting to tourism, polar bears are up against an agonizingly familiar series of threats that endanger thousands of species worldwide. But polar bears, which have evolved since the late Pleistocene in one of the planet's most inhospitable environments, must also negotiate an overarching obstacle to their survival: melting sea ice. As the evidence of global warming increases, ice that the bears depend on to help supply food and shelter is literally vanishing under their paws. Today, the iconic polar bear represents the biggest canary in the coldest gold mine, a warning about the tragic consequences of humanity's grip on the planet.

To talk about animals, or our encounters with animals, as this book does, and to do so without addressing the formidable changes that are taking place would be folly, if not dishonesty. Whatever its outcome, the debate over the polar bear's plight underscores how climate change presents a new challenge to conservation in the twenty-first century.[2] It has already affected half of the world's wild species—thousands of plants and animals, their breeding, distribution, abundance, and overall survival—by pushing them to higher elevations or latitudes, by altering mating patterns and driving plants to bloom earlier. Perhaps nowhere are these trends more obvious than in the Arctic, which is warming three to five times faster than the rest of the globe on average.

Contrary to its perceived image as a wasteland of snow, ice, and permafrost, the Arctic is a fecund ecosystem that pops alive in the summer and provides feeding grounds and way stations for hundreds of species, both terrestrial and marine: Arctic fox to zooplankton, alga to walrus. Specially adapted marine mammals like the ringed seal and tiny terrestrial mammals like the collared lemming eke out a living where other animals cannot.

The future is far from clear, but bad omens are taking shape for certain Arctic animals. Diminishing sea ice affects everything in the ocean's food chain, from small invertebrates to seals. Warming tundra alters the landscape, including lichen cover and moose forage. Birds that commute from all over the world to mate, nest, and molt now find that spring arrives earlier than they do. Bowhead whales that migrate from Baja, terns en route from Antarctica, and caribou that cross the Brooks Range converge on this open-air market only to find that the food aisles have been moved—farther north, offshore—or are gone entirely. Insect items that used to be in the tundra section in, say, June, are absent by mid-May. Subarctic species, both plants and animals, are expanding northward. Those already at the margins, like red phalaropes, dunlins, or Arctic foxes, have nowhere else to go.

Plants and animals that evolved over the past eight hundred thousand years to live in or visit this icy world now must readjust to shifting realities—or perish. Many of them may be able to adjust, and some would even benefit from a warmer climate. For others, a balmier world means difficulties if not doom. Birds like the king eider and black guillemot are already being forced to adopt new feeding, nesting, and mating routines because many insects hatch earlier now. The Canadian government recently listed a herd of Peary caribou as at risk, partly because later fall freezes have caused animals to break through thin ice and drown during their annual trip across the frozen twenty-five-mile-wide Dolphin and Union Straight that separates the mainland from Victoria Island.

Ice-dependent mammals in particular are suffering because of sea ice loss in the past few decades. With predictions that the Arctic will be seasonally ice free earlier than previously thought, the not-so-distant future looks bleak—and not just for polar bears. Ringed seals, bearded seals, walruses, narwhals, bowheads, and belugas as well will inhabit uninviting environments.

The ice-free summer of '04 was particularly disquieting, because near-shore sea ice is critical to jumpstarting the Arctic summer feeding frenzy. (Sea ice comes in many forms, including floating pack ice and shore-fast ice. Each harbors its own ecological niches.) That frenzy begins with the return of the sun in mid-March, heralding spring. Over the next few months, shore-fast and multiyear sea ice begins to break up, and light that infiltrates its edges provokes ice algae to bloom in sheets hanging from floes. Phytoplankton, another crucial strand in life's web, also starts to grow, enriching the water with dozens of varieties of tiny, drifting, plant-like, one-celled organisms.

An explosion of life follows: invertebrates like worms, bivalves like clams and filter feeders like brittle stars multiply on the shallow offshore sea shelf, gorging on phytoplankton and ice algae after they bloom and sink. In turn, different kinds of zooplankton, including shrimp-like crustaceans called copepods, proliferate, attracting grazers to the invertebrate smorgasbord: bottom-feeding waterfowl like spectacled eiders, copepod-chomping fish like Arctic cod, and clam-munching mammals like walruses all congregate to take advantage of the fleeting bounty. The floating ice is literally a moveable feast—until it dissolves or recedes so far offshore that the waters underneath deepen too much for bottom feeders to reach their preferred foods.

A scientific icebreaker crew gathering micro-invertebrate samples and measuring ocean temperature and salinity saw what would become a recurring, disturbing sight: abandoned walrus calves. First one motherless calf, then another, then a pair, and ultimately nine different walrus toddlers approached the ship during its voyage, each one barking incessantly. They were less than two years old, and normally would have been near their mothers in order to nurse. Though the scientists were wary about anthropomorphizing, the animals' distress was obvious. With each sighting the crew got more upset—but the Marine Mammal Protection Act prohibited them from interfering.

"None of us had ever seen anything like this before," a crewmember said.

Walruses normally "haul up" on and dive for clams and crabs from near-shore ice platforms above the shallow, narrow continental shelf that separates the shoreline from the deeper open sea. Calves normally wait on or near this floating ice for their mothers to return. Adult walruses can dive more than six hundred feet deep to forage, but even if there had been floes where the researchers saw the calves, the ocean floor was nearly ten thousand feet down.

Warmer water clearly sealed the fate of the nine walrus calves in an ice-free sea. "We knew these animals were goners," one researcher said.

Walruses are by no means alone in being ice-loving ("pagophilic")—or being in trouble as that substance thins and retreats. Startling observations of drowned polar bears in 2004 (the same low-ice year the walrus orphans were seen) suggest that even ursine marathon swimmers cannot negotiate the growing gaps ;between ice floes and shore. Bearded and ringed seals, which are the polar bear's main sustenance, also make their increasingly precarious living along the edges of moving pack ice: diving for fish, pupping on the floes, and creating blowholes to secretly surface and breathe. Polar bears, in turn, stalk seals by day, waiting near these holes, ready to pounce. If predictions of further sea ice reduction come true, narwhals, belugas, bowhead whales, and other more seasonally ice-dependent animals could see their food sources float farther out to sea—or disappear entirely.

The consequences will ripple up and down the Arctic marine food chain.

During one of his nightly patrols, Alaska oil field security guard Bill Petersen saw what looked like a dogfight of sorts. He probably did not realize he was documenting a symptom of off-kilter change when he pulled out a video recorder and taped an unusual occurrence near Prudhoe Bay on Alaska's North Slope: the predation of an Arctic fox by a larger red fox.

Petersen's video captured a fight to the death. The red fox chased the white Arctic fox through a parking lot, then clamped its neck and shook it until the animal became still. The next scene showed a triumphant red fox carrying the limp carcass to a patch of snow, where it proceeded to devour its canine relative.

It is not unusual to see red foxes and Arctic foxes mingling around Prudhoe Bay, but to the best of anyone's knowledge, nobody has ever watched a similar killing.

Just as climate scientists warn that it is impossible to determine global climate trends by any single event—like Hurricane Katrina or a heat wave in Europe—biologists caution against generalizations based on an observation like drowning polar bears, walrus orphans, or even a red fox eating an Arctic fox.

Still, the fox-on-fox killing is one of many incidents of unusual animal behavior that appear to be popping up around the terrestrial Arctic. As signs of climate change have become more pronounced, warmer temperatures have made higher latitudes hospitable for some subarctic species. During the past fifteen to twenty years, scientists have witnessed a northward movement in the range of red foxes, which will evict Arctic foxes from their dens. Because the red fox is about twice as big as the seven-pound Arctic fox, with lankier legs and a bigger jaw, it is likely to out-compete its counterpart.

If, due to shrinking sea ice, more Arctic foxes are forced to forage on land and more red foxes move northward, this greater population density will help spread rabies and canine distemper. A similar northward shift of Chronic Wasting Disease or parasites could affect caribou, musk oxen, and moose.

Arctic foxes play a crucial role in the terrestrial ecosystem through symbiotic relationships with snowy owls, jaegers, and endangered Steller's eiders, and through preying on lemmings and voles, which ultimately affects the sedges, lichens, forbs, grasses, and mosses that sustain herbivores. As with any system, a single disturbance can trigger a cascade of changes.

In northern Norway, Arctic foxes, snowy and short-eared owls, rough-legged buzzards, and lemmings live intertwined lives, their populations rising and falling in predictable cycles. Lemmings in particular are known for impressive bursts of reproduction. Their numbers also tend to crash every four years, for reasons that have produced dozens of theories but no agreement among experts.

Arctic foxes thrive during lemming booms, birthing up to sixteen kits when the rodent feast is in full swing. Snowy owls also dine on lemmings and peak when those are plentiful. They fiercely protect their nests and are big and vicious enough to keep foxes away. Other ground-breeders like Steller's eiders and sandpipers have learned the value of owl protection and often nest near them, increasing their own rate of survival.

Here's where climate change seems to disrupt the dance of species: lemmings feed on the forbs, sedges, and grasses the tundra yields—but their habitat is transforming quickly and profoundly. Shrubs now grow farther north. Warmer temperatures also evaporate many Arctic lakes, which dries out tundra and replaces the plants lemmings love to eat. Lemmings do not hibernate, and they rely on the insulation of snow burrows and tunnels to survive. If predicted climate changes in the Arctic bring milder winters with frequent thawing and freezing episodes, more lemmings and voles will die, and small rodents may not rebound as easily from their regular population crashes.

As the five-inch-long lemmings go, so goes the food chain. As lemming numbers drop, so do the numbers of snowy owls. Foxes are emboldened to raid goose nests when owl guardians are not present, and so on up and down the ladder of relationships.

Scenes like the videotaped fox fight and lemming-deprived red foxes pillaging bird nests may simply be first alarm signs from the continent's unraveling edge. A scientist for the Wildlife Conservation Society aptly summed up the dilemma: "It's like an opening salvo in what will increasingly be true in the rest of the world."

FUR

The Fawn's Eyes

RICHARD NELSON

Twenty-five degrees, calm, and clear. January sun lays a tender apricot blush on the snowfields of Kluska Mountain. My boots hiss softly in the deep powder. A week of snow has concentrated deer along the shore, where there's less accumulation under the big coastal trees, and close by, piles of kelp washed onto the beach provide a ready source of food.

After leaving the boat in a tiny cove this morning, my dog Keta and I came across a good-size buck, lean and bony from the rut, feeding on snarls of seaweed. There were two raw, pale spots on his forehead—roots of the antlers he'd recently shed in the nearby woods or muskegs. Those bare spots brought back childhood memories of an old Norwegian man our family sometimes visited on weekends. One of his fingers was a stump, neatly healed around the exposed end of the bone, so it looked like a button surrounded by pink flesh.

We left the buck, hiked down the shore, and soon encountered a lone doe standing just above the driftwood, then a doe and fawn who ran when we stepped noisily on a patch of gravel exposed by the ebbing tide. When I imitated a fawn's call, the doe reappeared at the trees' edge, fixed her eyes and ears on us, stretched out her neck, and called back in a low, soft voice, like the gentlest mooing of a cow, barely audible above the surging waves. Then she stared intently toward us, as if she expected a fawn to appear and follow her. Seeing only these two strangers, she finally turned, angled up the steep bank, and vanished without looking back. Now we've hiked a quarter mile along the beach without seeing more deer, but I expect some in a broad, crescent-shaped cove around the next point. Sure enough: two fawns and a doe. Moving very slowly, using boulders and driftwood logs for concealment, we sneak closer. Then, while all three deer are busy feeding, heads down amid kelp mounds, I step with Keta into the open.

During cold weather and snow, our blacktails become less vigilant and seem to abandon their normal wariness. If you keep absolutely still until they relax, move while they're not watching, and gradually let yourself become a visible part of the surroundings, they'll sometimes accept your intrusion and act as if you no longer matter. This peculiarity would make them vulnerable to predators or to hunters with exceptional patience, but the risk must be outweighed by the survival value of keeping calm and conserving energy. In any case, all three deer hold us in a protracted stare, then gradually settle back to feeding.

After a while, one of the fawns ambles up into the woods and disappears, but the other fawn stays behind, close to the doe, indicating this pair is a mother and her offspring. Some young ones rejoin their mothers after the rut, and some are more independent. Watching the deer move around makes Keta so excited I worry she'll bolt after them, so I ease into a crouch and gently stroke her fur. From the way her body trembles, I wonder that it doesn't hum like an electric wire. Holding out one hand, I give her the signal to lie down on lava bedrock washed bare by the tide. She obeys reluctantly, her attention still fastened on the deer.

After I've gone a ways toward the animals, I slowly turn to check on her, and for a moment she seems to have vanished. Then I realize my mistake. Her black fur perfectly matches the lava, the white ring around her neck resembles a patch of snow, and her bright, blazing eyes gleam like ice crystals clinging to the rocks. Over the next twenty minutes, I work closer to the doe and fawn, taking one step at a time, letting my presence soak in. Keta holds absolutely still, but at intervals I reach a hand behind my back and reaffirm the signal to lie down.

Both deer are standing at the abrupt edge between snow and sand, the highest reach of last night's tide, rooting around in a snarl of kelp, pulling out flaccid strands and chewing them up into their mouths like cold spaghetti. Early on, they were occasionally struck by moments of fear, but while I've come closer they've grown more relaxed, as if I'm just another deer or an irrelevant, innocuous, movable object. The distance between us narrows to fifty feet, thirty, twenty, fifteen. Then I stop, keep very still, and watch.

The doe is medium sized for an island blacktail, three feet tall at the shoulder, probably about a hundred pounds, sleek furred, smooth, and round—unusually fat for midwinter. The fawn looks about half her size, with long, dainty legs and a body not much larger than Keta's. I watch the rise and fall of their chests, the blinking of their eyes, the muscles working in their jaws.

After some minutes, they bend toward each other until their noses touch, and the fawn licks his mother's face. She leans down, closing her eyes while the tiny pink tongue caresses her fur, ranging from cheek to forehead. But shortly, another impulse takes over: the doe shunts away, lifts a foreleg, and rests it on her fawn's back, asserting her claim to the kelp. In response, the fawn steps a few yards away and begins to feed again.

Then, without apparent reason or forewarning, the little one lifts his head, funnels his ears, and reaches his muzzle toward me—all in curiosity, without a trace of fear. He angles toward my right side, turns sharply, and comes straight my way. I have no time to think, except to wonder if I might try to touch him should he come within reach. His hooves on a patch of frozen gravel sound crisp and brittle as wrinkling paper.

The approaching fawn keeps his forelegs angled slightly outward, as if he might abruptly swerve away, but he comes on without wavering and pauses only when he reaches the edge of a shallow tidewater pool a few feet wide. For a moment his image is splendidly reflected, as if there were a fawn on the shore and another in the sky.

Then his hoof touches the pond, breaking the mirror, and he steps across, halting about three feet away. The pale tips of his ears are no higher than my waist. He looks up into my face and seems all eyes: black and wet and shining eyes; eyes filled with sunlight and snow, dark rocks and shimmering water; eyes like the clear, limitless dome of a midnight sky; eyes that take my image into the fawn and spin me through the networks of his mind, as my own eyes have brought the fawn inside me.

At the island's edge, in the glare of winter sun, amid the sounds of surging waters, with the breeze eddying between us, the fawn and I share a moment of pure bewilderment.

After a few minutes, the little deer straightens and turns, crosses deliberately in front of me, and circles to my side, keeping the same distance. I could now reach out to touch him, but have no inclination to do so and feel sure he'd startle if I tried. When the fawn stops, I glance back at Keta, still crouched against the rocks, tense as a wishbone bent to the shattering point.

Slowly now, the fawn moves around behind me—and there he collides with the bitter, drifting pall of my scent. Almost involuntarily, he winces back. He shoves his muzzle into the scent once more, like someone who tastes a sizzling pepper twice to affirm a sensation that barely seems possible. He recoils, turns end for end, follows his earlier tracks around to my front side, and pauses to stare at me like a deceived child. Then he struts away, flagging the bright underside of his tail, a perfect miniature of an adult deer making a frightened but honorable retreat.

Oddly, when the fawn reaches his mother's side, he relaxes and bends down to pick at the kelp. But the watchful doe has taken on the fear he seems to have forgotten, although she acts as if it had nothing to do with me. Her body stiffens; her ears shift one way and the other; then she turns and leads him up the beach, across the snow-covered driftwood, into the tangled shroud of forest.

I wait a moment to be sure they've gone, then signal for Keta. She dashes up, snuffles the fresh-tracked snow, wags her tail, nuzzles my hand, fidgets, rubs against my side and looks bright-eyed into my face, then stares toward the place where the deer vanished, begging me to follow. I kneel down and give her a hug, whispering thanks in her ear.

My body is filled with energy and elation. I feel joy and gratitude for this winter day, this wild country, this blessed companionship of animals.

On the Hunt

DREW POGGE

H e appeared to me near the river, alone in the cold, and stood watching as I skied closer. *Mangy-looking thing*, I thought.

But I was alone, too. The backcountry is my sanctuary from humanity. It's all that is wild. So I sometimes ski along the winter river, its high banks rimmed by intricate, gnarled cornices of snow, hoping, for a while, to be wild too. And that day, he was waiting.

He watched me, but didn't run. Like the river flowing over thick cascades of moon-colored pancake ice, the way he moved was inimitable, inevitable. He lowered his head and shifted his weight from foot to foot contemplatively. And then he stood upright, brown-edged ears erect. He turned deliberately and dashed up the steep fifty-foot riverbank; the only clue to his passing was a trail of small prints in the snow. Intrigued, I followed.

Clambering up the boulder-strewn bank in pursuit, I wondered why he was alone. Maybe he was hunting. Maybe he was a vagabond. Maybe he just wanted to explore the uninterrupted reach of the mountains in peace. *Maybe we shared more than a moment by a river*, I thought.

At the top of the bank he was waiting, sitting in the afternoon shadow of a large boulder with his bushy tail curled around his haunches. His expression was that of a comic sage, a Chaplinesque monk. He had quiet brown eyes, curious and skeptical, cynical and proud. But he didn't run.

He just looked at me and sat, while I breathed heavily and looked back at him.

Alone, it becomes easy to see and hear things. The river sounds different. It's softer and duller, like shouting into a pillow. Snow speaks as well. It squeaks and whispers in lost Arctic tongues. All around is an unsoiled beauty that defies human constructs. Ambition, expectation, and disappointment fade to the clarity of frigid survival. Winter immaculate.

I watched him sitting by the boulder, and I was afraid. He was small, but powerful. Each movement was efficient, each twitch deliberate. Even from a distance, I could see his lean, muscular form rippling under a thick winter coat. Glossy and oaken, highlighted by streaks of blond and chocolate sepia, he was elegant and commanding. Stepping up the mountain, he looked back, smiling through parted lips and exposed incisors. He was a beautiful fright.

Pacing in small circles, he kept his head low, and his eyes never left mine as I stepped into my skis. He was beckoning, demanding that I follow. Bending over to secure my bindings, I was conflicted, uneasy, and awed, and I rationalized.

It was just one little coyote after all. I could spear him with a ski pole if he attacked. I could beat him, stab him, kill him. He would lie in the snow, melting into a bloody stain like a bowl of spilt punch, and his brown eyes would blacken until they demanded nothing, and The Order of Things would be restored. This is what I thought as I began skiing, following the coyote. But he didn't attack, and I didn't kill. He walked, and I skied, and we climbed the mountain together.

He kept a considerable distance between us, but never strayed. And he set a good track—not too steep, not too exposed. He knew this mountain well. But he paused for a moment near the top of the climb. His delicate muzzle probed the sky like an oscillating sieve, a million scent molecules percolating in an instant. They told him everything about this place. About me.

He changed course, veering from a logical route that would lead us to the summit.

This is the place he will leave me, I thought. *I'll ski, and he'll live and everything will be the same.* But he trotted a short distance and then he turned, and his direct gaze beckoned me once more.

I don't know why I followed. I have never followed moose or deer, or ravens or eagles. They're remembered only in passing, novelties that somehow enrich the day with wild flavor. They're talked about over dinner for one or two sentences and then forgotten. So even as I skied behind, watching his lithe form move smoothly over the snow, I asked myself why *I* was there. And I knew then how it must have been, when man first found himself in wild company. I trusted him. I trusted his innate competence. *Perhaps it wasn't we who tamed the beast,* I thought, *but the other way round.*

The coyote and I worked together to the ridge. He was waiting again as I crested the final climb, with the peak only yards away. Sitting innocently on the snow, my guide was composed and curious, and his thick tail slowly swept over the snow in easy pendulum strokes. We stared again at one another for a moment, judging. Then I shuffled slightly and he startled. Twitching to his feet, he trotted—slender paws drumming in two-four time—to the true summit. There he turned into a north wind that blew his coat into waves of earthy color, and our eyes met once more. He bared his teeth and put back his head and seemed to laugh. And then he was gone.

On the scalloped, ridge-top slab, his tracks remained only a short while. Wind-driven snow eroded them in moments, and they faded like dawn frost from a windowpane. I watched them lose warmth, lose definition, and finally become lost altogether. The last physical reminder of the coyote blew south, and I was alone again on the mountain. Preparing for my downhill run, I thought of him. *How strange.* Looking over the edge, to the fifteen hundred vertical feet of snow and slope below, I could faintly make out our tracks. *It was a good route,* I thought. *It was a good climb.*

I pushed off and skied over a series of gentle benches, and where the slope rolled over steeply, I slowed to see what lay below. In that moment, the snow didn't speak. It shrieked—a wrenching, tearing battle scream. A crack arced between my feet, and, like a great jaw opening to reveal fang upon icy fang, the avalanche broke free. I lunged uphill and watched as the entire mountainside fractured. The scream became a deep, jet-engine rumble as sofa-size blocks of snow liquefied and sailed into the abyss. A hunk of pure white flesh was ripped from the body of the peak, and from the wound bled bare black earth. Perched safely above the avalanche crown, I breathed a sigh of relief as the slide slowed and the snow settled, and it was then that I saw it.

My intended ascent path was gone—an exposed rocky scar. There is little doubt that the avalanche would have taken me. Not far away, where the coyote stopped and sniffed for a moment, our tracks remained, climbing safely away from the slide. He had known.

Some say I'm a fool for skiing alone. "You could have died," they say. "What were you doing out there anyway?" But it's difficult to explain—escaping my own humanity or pursuing some vague idea of wild nature. So I say I was following a coyote, and some nod, as though they often follow coyotes up mountains. Most don't understand. They say the coyote was probably running away from me, afraid and confused. Some even say he was waiting for the avalanche to take me, so that he could scavenge my remains.

But I prefer to think that he was just a solitary coyote searching for something, as I was searching. And there, by the syrupy winter river, we found one another, and found in one another the very things we each so quietly sought. With my trust and fearful admiration, he found in me a kindred winter traveler, and I found in him a steward of freedom and true wild spirit. With wary understanding, we climbed a mountain together. And he helped me live.

In the vastness of the mountains, a north wind ruffles the enviable coat of a coyote grinning through bared incisors. His eyes are wild and beautiful, frightening and kind. And muzzle to the sky, he's laughing.

The Wolverine Way

DOUGLAS H. CHADWICK

To catch wolverines for a radio-tracking study in Montana's Glacier National Park, we picked out spots where paw prints converged in the winter backcountry and set about building stout box traps from spruce and fir logs. The walls were eight inches thick, but that didn't keep some of these animals from tearing their way out in a matter of hours. If one was still there when we lifted the lid a notch to peer in, the opening instantly filled with a blur of claws like crampons, teeth that can crunch a moose femur, and deep, rattling growls—Wolverine for, "Hope you don't need your face, tame boy, because I'm going to take it *off*."

Wolverines sometimes force grizzlies away from a kill, which, we can all agree, is a badass thing to do when you weigh twenty-five to thirty-five pounds. Members of our research team often talked about the baddest of all, a wolverine's wolverine: M3. During the course of the research, which began in 2002 and continues today, I'd followed signals from his radio through remote valleys in the park, but never glimpsed him. Oh, he's big, they told me, heavier than his dad, M1 (who lays claim to the center of Glacier and to three girlfriends there). Most wolverines are explosive inside a trap, but they said that M3 went completely nuclear, that trying to jab him with a syringe-tipped pole would demolish your nerves, that it took twice the expected drug dose to knock him down. They once found him ripping and chewing his way *into* a closed trap, not to reach the bait but to get at a rival, old M6, who had been caught earlier.

Like the other wolverines in the project, M3 made his home in *Mistakis* (Backbone of the World), the Blackfeet Indian name for the cavalcade of peaks that makes up modern-day Glacier, adjoining Waterton Lakes National Park in Alberta, and the country bordering those two reserves. Enormous as the landscape seems, it is just one link in a long, lovely, untamed, and still mostly unbroken chain of refuge and inspiration running from New Mexico to northern Canada—the Rocky Mountains, which divide North America's waters and shape much of its climate east and west. More in keeping with the Blackfeet vision, many refer to the Rockies as the Spine of the Continent.

Through midsummer's flare of wildflowers and midwinter blizzards that piled snow as deep as twenty feet, M3 spent his first year rambling the territories of his parents. As a yearling, he probed farther north, pushing into M6's turf along the park's Belly River drainage, closer to Canada. A year later, he owned the place, and M6 was gone. Then M3 expanded his range, mated with a female on its eastern edge, and fathered a son, M20.

Radio-tracking amid towering crags that block signals is tough to start with, and much of M3's swelling territory was especially hard to reach. We'd go months without hearing his electronic *cheeps*. But in 2007, the team separately captured M3 and his second son, M23, now a yearling, and replaced their radios with satellite collars. Programmed to record GPS locations every five minutes, the high-tech devices would create a picture of the wolverines' movements in unprecedented detail. The catch was that we had to live-trap the animals again to download data from this particular type of collar.

We got lucky. We caught M3 in the Many Glacier Valley just as the March snow was beginning to soften and the river ice was breaking up. I skied in to help handle the animal and had my first look at Mr. Badass himself. He was as big and snarly as promised. And yet as he faced us down in his glossy, rich chocolate coat with russet streaks, he was, above all, beautifully, indomitably wild. He was perfect.

Other wolverines we'd monitored traveled day and night at a relentless pace, keeping it up even as they scaled almost sheer cliffs and cols, waltzed across avalanche chutes and padded along overhanging cornices. How about M3? Once upon a time, field naturalists would gather around a warm, flickering fire in the evening. Now they huddle around the glow of a computer screen. Here's our team looking over his locations, downloaded earlier in the day and superimposed on a topographic map:

"Holy $#&@! He summited Cleveland [the park's highest peak at 10,466 feet]!"

"And he did the last 4,900 feet straight up in ninety minutes."

"Yuh. In frickin' February."

"All *right*, we've got him traveling with M23 for a while first. Identical times and locations."[3]

"After climbing Cleveland he goes way up into Waterton Lakes. First, he crosses into British Columbia, then into Alberta. No wonder we couldn't find him. His territory's several hundred square miles."

Both this project and another long-running study in the Greater Yellowstone Ecosystem found not only adult wolverines consistently roaming within huge territories, but also younger animals loping off much farther, exploring whole new landscapes when they sought out homes of their own. Meanwhile, in the lower forty-eight states, wolverine habitat continues to be fragmented. Developments reach farther and higher into untamed stretches. The animal's remarkable nose leads too many into steel-jawed traps—including those set for other predators such as coyotes or bobcats—along the expanding webwork of roads. And wolverines have grown more rare than grizzlies and wolves—in fact, so rare that they are being considered for listing as threatened or endangered south of Canada.

Wolverines don't need a few secure areas to survive. They need *lots* of secure areas—big ones—and healthy corridors of protected land in between to link populations and the genes they carry. The most intact strongholds left for North America's large native animals are right here in the Rockies—the continent's spine. What happens to freedom of movement when a spinal column gets fractured? How do we keep folks from logging, mining, drilling, or bulldozing ever deeper into the core until they finally bust this land's back?

As the wolverine becomes better known at last, it adds a fierce emphasis to the message that every bear, wolf, lynx, and other major carnivore keeps giving: if the living systems we choose to protect aren't large and strong and interconnected, then we aren't really conserving them. Not for the long term. Not with some real teeth in the scenery. We're just talking about saving nature while we settle for something less wild.

A Romance

JO GOING

I was sitting cross-legged on the ground, painting bighorn sheep on Mount Rundle, which rises like an evocation above Banff in the Canadian Rockies. As so often happens in my encounters with wildlife, I had rounded a bend in the trail, and there was the herd, calmly browsing between the rocks. Keeping a respectful distance, I slowly and evenly situated myself with my paints, entering into that communion between brush and wild animal that has so shaped my art and my thought.

I have learned to paint wild animals quickly, one sure brushstroke indicating muscle, bone, movement, spirit. As the presence of wild sheep, in cadmium yellow and cobalt blue, wandered onto my paper, I was sinking into that inner dialogue that closes the space between self and other. The brush caressingly traced spiraling horns, reflecting the curve of the glacial river far below. Shapes of fur gradually transformed into color and light.

Possibly from mere curiosity, or responsibility, one of the largest rams—his bearing confident—stared at me with such intensity that I felt his questioning. Who was the pink, clothed being in the midst of his home and family? With no hesitation in his steps, he approached with declarative affirmation, stopped within inches, and, bending down, put his soft nose gently on top of my small hand and its paintbrush, sniffing. Meditatively still, I felt the moist warmth of his very breath on my own flesh.

With that distinctive look, that seemingly second sight that is the gaze of wild animals, he turned his head to survey the full extent of me. I could count his eyelashes, and stared back into that golden eye, my own reflection a transparency suspended within the slitlike rectangular pupil. Just one, even gentle, nudge from those powerful horns, and I would have tumbled back over the precipice.

But his intention was otherwise. Perhaps from some instinct of herd initiation, one more female, if a bit unusual, to safeguard and protect, he lifted his leg and urinated, marking me with his scent. The rich, heavy smell of fur and animal closeness became an invisible blanket that defined the space of our mutual presence. After considering me one last time, he stepped away, paused, and, looking back in invitation to follow, walked over the rim of the trail. He then disappeared from view, the herd, except for me, following.

It was all so matter-of-fact in the moments of occurrence that I took the meeting with an almost casual acceptance of the ordinary. It was not until he vanished out of sight that I felt his presence viscerally, smelled again his warm breath on my hand, and knew I had been touched by a god.

Now, forever, there are two spirals of golden light growing from my forehead, the wildness inside me in calm surrender to the place of my life in the journey home.

Elusive Lynx

CAROL KAYNOR

few years ago, as the hare cycle[4] was just on the far side of peaking in interior Alaska, I saw an unfamiliar animal running across the end of our road. At first I had no idea what it was. It was as big as a dog but ran like a cat, and I puzzled over it for a moment until I realized, with a sense of awe, that I'd seen my first lynx.

Some days later, as my husband, my neighbor Bonnie, and I were driving home, our headlights illuminated the tail end of the lynx just ahead of us. It bounded down our road for a little while in a funny, up-and-down gait before bolting off into the bushes. The rest of the way home, we talked excitedly about the encounter. We live in Goldstream Valley, a bit out of Fairbanks but certainly not far enough out to be considered real wilderness. To see a lynx in our little mushers' subdivision was something quite out of the ordinary. It became the main topic of the neighborhood.

Bonnie and I run sled dogs together, and the next time I was at her house to take out a team, she spoke enthusiastically about setting out a snare for the lynx. I asked her if she wanted it for the pelt, and she said yes, but also, she'd eat it. I was surprised. In my ignorance, I thought all carnivores were not good eating. No, she said; she'd had lynx before. "It's delicious."

Bonnie was born and raised in Alaska and brought up to hunt, fish, and trap. Her father expected her to be just as tough and capable as her two brothers. Bonnie's parents are taxidermists, and she has handled dead animals all her life. She has studied the tracks and habits of live ones, as I think all good hunters must do. Many times she and I have come back from running teams and she's asked me if I saw the tracks on the trail that day. They might be moose, maybe fox or dog, or marten or lynx, and she would have identified what kind of animal made them as she went by at eighteen miles an hour. I'd have been lucky to notice there were tracks.

I love woods and water, and wild animals of all sorts, but eat no meat except seafood. I don't trap, I don't hunt, and I only kill fish. I look with fascination and appreciation at the variety of stuffed and mounted animals scattered throughout Bonnie's house—sheep and buffalo heads, a raccoon, a gray fox, a ferret. I don't spend too much time thinking about how they got there. Most of the time, our two disparate philosophies run quietly and peacefully counter to each other, without any need to find common ground. We have enough common ground in the dogs, and in loving the woods. We work for hours together on the dog trails—grooming, brushing, clearing. I pull on leaning spruces as Bonnie fells them with her brush ax. Bonnie cleans up behind me as I mow down encroaching willows. We dig obsessively around the roots of a big stump that has snagged our trail-grooming drag one too many times. With Bonnie's ax and my mattock and chainsaw, we say we are the deadliest stump-murderers in the valley.

The lynx was a challenge. Bonnie had been just as enchanted as I to see it in our neighborhood. We were in accord on that. Our accord parted ways when she began to talk of trapping it. I didn't know how to reconcile my respect for her lifestyle, even if I didn't like the idea of killing, with my desire to keep this particular lynx alive. I wanted to say to her, simply, "If you trap it, none of the rest of us will ever be able to see that lynx again." I wanted our little neighborhood to be sacrosanct, so that animals would be safe and therefore more visible. I wanted the lynx to find haven here.

I said nothing, and hoped the lynx would stay out of her snare. I believe Bonnie may have known how I felt without my having to put it into words. I don't know if it would have stopped her. We negotiate many of our differences in silence. She didn't catch the lynx, I do know that. She would not have hidden it from me. But it disappeared. It may have starved in the waning hare cycle, or perhaps it went somewhere else seeking a way to survive. Maybe someone else trapped it. It is easier not to know what happened to the lynx than to think of seeing it stuffed and mounted in Bonnie's living room.

In my yard is a dog Bonnie bred but would not have kept. To Bonnie, this dog is useless, a waste of time and dog food. I saw something else and brought her home. Now, Kluane comes with me back to Bonnie's house and we run her with our other dogs. Bonnie wishes I had not taken Kluane, and sometimes complains, but she deals with it. In Bonnie's house are the bodies of animals I would not have trapped, and food in her freezer that I will not eat. She shoots squirrels, and I teach gray jays to eat from my hand. It is an uneven partnership, and sometimes the ground we walk together is a little bit unstable. We both love the land and we are loyal friends to each other, so we've found a way to manage. I feed my dogs the moose bones she gives me, and she doesn't try to talk me into eating moose myself.

A long time ago I was given a beautiful white and silver fur hat. Though I rarely wear it nowadays, preferring my musher's hat with its synthetic fleece and nylon, I sometimes dig out the fur hat when it's really cold. It is probably arctic fox, but for all I know about furs, it could just as well be lynx.

Heart Underfoot

STEVE KAHN

There are places on the trail that hold ghosts. Places that haunt and beckon us. Trees or fields, ridges or rocks that trap us. Forever dust and deadfall, the slow snake of path ahead, curving, shrinking into nothingness.

For me, one such place lies where an old jeep trail that links Farewell Lake to Farewell Station passes near the west end of John Lake. As small patches of boreal forest go, it is unremarkable. If you are walking with the morning sun at your back, something eases you down the rutted track—a gentle downhill, and an earth pull that makes you believe you could walk on endlessly. Dwarf birch gives way to tall grass as you approach the stand of white spruce hunched at the bottom. To the right the conifers are larger than most in the area. A deep game trail winds under their boughs, up from the edge of the lake. You can't see the water, or how the lake wraps itself, moatlike, around three sides of a steep ridge. But you feel it. I have passed this place in the boot-sole sink of spring, known the dust and mosquito buzz of midsummer, the crisp flirtation of autumn, and the cold that follows.

In my history here, there is sadness too. Even the red squirrel's bark loses its edge as the sound weaves down through the boughs, more a lament than a scold. Spruce cone detritus forms random, soggy piles beneath the tallest trees. The needle of my soul's barometer sinks and a slow, counterclockwise spin begins. There is a graying at the edges of things: the gnarled roots of an alder, a withered bolete abandoned on a branch, the shape of my hand.

It was the late 1970s and I was doing what young, single, wilderness lodge caretakers did in Alaska during the winter: trap. There was a rhythm to most days that I came to expect and love: noting each morning's first sensation of cool air on my face; looking up to the mosaic swirl of metal springs on the underbelly of the upper bunk; glancing to the cassette deck mounted on a wooden shelf, surrounded by the little boxes containing my favorite tunes, all within arm's reach; feeling my left shoulder pressing against the chestnut-hued log wall. And, as if I were the one to introduce sound and smell to the world each morning, there was the creaking of the plank floor as I walked over to the barrel stove and the crackle of dried spruce, followed by the perk and aroma of coffee. In many ways the setting was idyllic. It seemed I was finally leading the life that I had dreamed about for so many years.

What I knew about trapping came from reading and from casual comments by outdoorsmen I'd met. My father, an avid hunter and fisherman, didn't want any part of trapping. He'd grown up on a farm in Wisconsin, and through most of his teenage years his parents raised mink. When his brothers left home to serve in the military during World War II, he was the one who fed the mink and cleaned their cages. He broke their necks and skinned them. He smelled the strong odor of confinement and felt the pain of their teeth sinking through leather gloves into the meat of fingers.

Under the hiss and brightness of a gas lantern I studied my dog-eared trapping manual. In the field, I studied harder. Much of what I read about animal behavior turned out to be true.

Beneath the protecting branches of a spruce tree, I spiked a stout, dry, seven-foot pole that ran diagonally from the ground and protruded eighteen inches past the tree. Called a pole set, it is a favorite of those working marten country. The trap and bait are placed on the upper end, and the marten, a tree climber, ascends the pole to reach the bait and consequently steps into the trap. The trap is secured lightly to the pole with a string, wire, or bent nail, and in the animal's struggles it drops off and swings clear, taking the marten with it. In cold weather the animals freeze quickly, usually in a few hours. That is how I had always found them. Dead and frozen.

But a Chinook wind had warmed the December air to above freezing. There was no need to stoke the barrel stove that morning to ensure a warm cabin upon my return. The strap-hinged, cotton batten–chinked door latched easily. Outside, my snowshoes rested on the brow tines of a huge set of moose antlers spiked to the front wall. I would not need the webbed, wooden frames on the hard-packed trail. I shouldered my pack and began walking.

Within the first thirty minutes I passed two sets with nothing in them, but ahead there was movement. Beneath the pole, a marten hung inches from the ground. There was a minklike grace to its form. Stretched out, the animal looked sleeker than the ones I had seen peering down from the branches of black spruce, their soft, round ears framing teddy bear faces. The jaws of the Victor No. 1 single spring held one front paw, its fine, ivory white claws emerging from the plush brown fur. I unbuckled the belt of my pack and shoulder-dipped and arm-tucked my way out from under the straps.

This was supposed to be my moment, a chance to confirm my membership in the fraternal order of mountain men. An opportunity to collect a token of manhood and some tangible proof that my time had not been wasted. Justification of existence on a primal level. But there was no thrill or sense of accomplishment, just a nagging pressure at my temples and a tightness in my chest.

The marten's efforts to escape came in waves; it was an amateur gymnast on the rings struggling to perfect a new move, then swinging to rest. I had read that a sharp blow with a stick across the nose would stun a small animal and it would die quickly once you stood on its chest. The kicking and squirming of the marten intensified when I approached it with my walking stick half cocked. The constant motion, the twirling of the furry mobile into new positions, made me check the first swing and the second.

Finally, I choked up on my surrogate club for more speed and accuracy and rapped the marten in the face.

Whether the blow was off angle or merely not hard enough, I don't know. The trap chain that was wired to the pole slipped several inches, and the animal's hind feet touched the ground. It lunged at me, jerking against the steel jaws that held its paw. I jumped back. My only recourse was to flail away with my stick like a man snuffing out a burning bush until the marten lay there, stunned and twitching. I stepped forward quickly, one foot on its chest.

There was a taste of iron in my mouth. *Please die. Please just let me kill you.* I cursed the steep and messy learning curve. I reprimanded myself, thinking I should have secured the trap chain better, positioned it farther up the pole so there was less chance of the marten touching the ground. I thought of the far too many squirrels and gray jays that had perished before I learned ways to hide my traps. And still, even with increased experience, there were unwanted deaths, remnants of fur, feathers, and blood.

We can learn a lot from reading, but there is nothing like experience. And there is no chronometer sensitive enough to measure the length of certain moments. Like the time I knelt a dozen feet away from a lynx, wiring a snare in the shape of a noose to the end of a long pole, and the only sound was the squeak of dry snow against my boots as I stood. Because a bullet hole will bring less money for the skin, because lynx die easily. Cat eyes upon me, the loop of wire slipped over the feline neck. Lift up, up, I told myself, and the full weight of its death was in my hands.

What I didn't learn from reading trapping manuals is that finding my place in the life and death cycles on which all natural systems depend would be hard. Courage to change comes in tiny increments, in admitting the difference between killing for food and killing for fur. For a while I tried to bridge that gap by eating the flesh of muskrat, beaver, and lynx. But I was eating the meat because of a self-imposed obligation to minimize waste, not because I relished the flavor. Though my culinary limitations were a factor, I never got past the greasy, sweet taste. Even though I sold the fur, I couldn't shake the thought that these creatures should be more than a commodity.

I quit trapping. Years passed and I came to live on another lake in remote Alaska, surrounded by different mountains. A neighbor to the east fed and photographed the animals; another to the west trapped and skinned them. One winter when I watched the easy gait of a westbound wolf, my heart lifted, then too quickly settled. I never heard the shot, but the voice of my neighbor was clear as he boasted over the VHF radio how he never had to leave his cabin, just picked up his rifle and opened the window.

Later I passed by the crumpled carcass, misshapen and bird-picked on the ice. The cold I felt was bone-and-muscle deep, and the ice I stood on was not the only thing that had buckled and fractured.

I continue to hunt and fish for food, but something has changed. Salmon and burbot are filleted closer to the bone. Grouse blood stains fingers that hold the bird a bit longer to feel its warmth, its softness. Its feathers, its feet, its weight are all a part of me, and I think of my parents, my wife, and my friends. As if joy were to the east and sadness to the west, I stand on a hillside exactly in between, feeling both.

The experts tell how to trap a marten. What they don't mention is if the snow is too soft or deep, the body of the marten beneath the foot settles away from the crushing pressure and that it is necessary to put even more weight on that leg to finish the job. They didn't tell me whether the beating was coming from under my foot or from my own chest or how someday I would sit next to my mother in the hospital waiting room while my father's guts were in the hands of a surgeon—how my mother's heart, for decades enlarged and beating irregularly, would feel as if in my own hands.

I sometimes look through my cabin window at the mountains and imagine a small creature held by steel jaws. I remember a tiny patch of earth just west of John Lake and how nobody told me, as I stood on that heart and stared straight ahead, that the pulse of the moment would last such a long time.

Spinster

LYNN DEFILIPPO

It's raining today and I'm glad of it, this cold, misty rain. The spinning wheel thrums, my foot pumps, and from a piece of super-fine qiviut I draw out my right hand and watch wool twist into yarn. I'm a lazy spinner. I want only the finest qiviut to spin now. I don't want to sort or clean or pick through my stash. I desire only to sit at the wheel and listen to its rhythmic pulse, admire the lustrous pearly brown slipping through my fingers. Left thumb and middle finger come together with the spinning length of yarn between them, then let go again. Touch and go, touch and go, ever so slightly controlling the twist. On occasion I pause, pick out a piece of tundra, a splinter of moss or twig, a long, wiry guard hair. The wheel turns. I dream of the past, the future; a heated flush rises up in me. I stop, reach for another piece. Such a satisfying and lonely craft. Around and around, my old Ashford Traditional spinning wheel turns and turns, making one endless cord. The flyer, sitting atop the maidenhead, spins as well and winds the single strand onto the bobbin. It takes a while to fill a bobbin with this thin qiviut single thread. In summer I spin only a small portion of the nicest pieces, freshly gathered, leaving the rest for winter.

I learned to spin some nine years ago from a woman in interior Alaska. Through dark woods of spruce along the Nenana River, I walked the trail to Lauralee's cabin. Watching her spin fiber into yarn looked magical and powerful, useful and beautiful. Thick skeins hung from the rafters in her log cabin; boxes and crates along one wall spilled over with a rainbow of handspun yarns. This was no wretched spinster hag of the Grimms' tales, no witch who turns girls to stone or bargains with maidens. This spinner ran sled dogs and guided big-game hunting trips and jet-boat safaris. We visited over tea, listened to the hiss of the wood fire, and her life was laid before me: guns leaning in a corner, winter gear and dog harnesses hanging on hooks by the door, a black bearskin tacked to the wall, windows overlooking the dog yard. A small creek next to her house provided water for the dyeing process, and beside it, a huge stainless-steel bowl sat atop a propane hot-dog cooker. From this cauldron, steaming skeins emerged in glorious purples, blues, and emerald greens, pulled from the dye bath on a long, sturdy stick. I loved that spot by the river, where my friend taught me her craft: first to knit, then spin, then dye the beautiful dog fur and wool yarns that are the trademark of a handful of Alaska spinners. I became one of them.

My home on the Seward Peninsula sits between the Bering Sea and the treeless, rolling foothills of the Kigluik range to the north. June is a glorious month here. The tundra comes alive with early grasses, willow buds, wildflowers, and migrating birds. In May and June, musk oxen congregate in herds with their newborn calves. Looking out from the kitchen window, I can scan the hills with binoculars and see these creatures forage on the southern slopes of two nearby mountains, just north of Nome. Yesterday I noted a herd of twenty below a remaining snow patch in a section of mountainside I've been eyeing for my next qiviut-picking hike. If only that grizzly sow and her yearling cubs hadn't killed a calf there two days ago, I'd be out now plucking sheets of qiviut from the willow branches.[5] Qiviut is the downy underfur of the musk ox, shed each spring and early summer. Some say it is the softest, lightest, warmest fiber in the world. Certainly it is the rarest. Protected by layers of guard hair and a long, coarse skirt that reaches almost to the ground, qiviut warms these ice age creatures during winters in the far northern reaches of North America. In summer it's common to see herds of fifteen or so musk oxen with six to seven calves. Sometimes that number swells to twenty to twenty-five musk oxen and as many as ten calves romping around hillsides fragrant with wildflowers. Combing the willows behind them as they graze, I often gather qiviut close to the musk oxen as they shed it. I try to keep my distance but can get greedy when I spot gossamer hanging in the willows. If the sun is at just the right angle, the qiviut fluffs reflect light. Following the shimmering trail, I'll be drawn from one spot to the next, filling up my scarves and sacks. So soft, so fine—did this piece come from a little calf? I muse, though I know it's not possible. Musk ox calves are born with dark-brown fuzz, a mix between underfur and outer guard hair. They will grow their qiviut insulation through their first winter and shed it the next year. Some hunks light as babies' breath—gleaming, cloudlike pieces the size of cookie sheets—I've collected from shedding bulls. In my visions I see myself approaching these imposing beasts and plucking the fiber as it dangles off them. Don't you want me to comb you, shaggy musk ox? Here—I'll relieve you of that too-hot coat; it looks so untidy. In reality I keep my distance, and they tolerate me.

Alone at the spinning wheel, I sometimes wish I had an apprentice, a girl. She could make the tea, do the bothersome task of winding the full bobbins onto the swift, tie the skeins, then wash and hang them. As we clean and sort, spin and ply this wild, gathered fiber into yarn, I'd remember the time a bull musk ox roared at me as I roamed, collecting qiviut just behind a browsing herd of cows and calves. The bull stood alone on the ridgeline above his large family and saw me advancing on them. He ran down the slope and roared twice, a thundering, deep-throated bellow that displayed his teeth. Respectfully, I retreated to my picking zone. Our stories would be spun into yarn and knit into hats, and I'd pass on my craft to another.

My husband, Kevin, loves to ramble around the country, observing animals, collecting shed antlers from caribou and reindeer, glassing for critters, hunting. Our first June living in Nome he returned from a hike with a plastic grocery bag full of newly shed qiviut. The next day we drove out into the country to get more. Musk oxen dotted the countryside while we filled our packs with this tundra gold. I dreamt of spinning skeins of the world's most exotic fiber, the fiber infused with land, sun, sky. Kevin, for his part, is a skilled wildcrafter, a man after my own heart. He only selects the best qiviut pieces, taking time to remove debris while in the field. His keen eye knows where the musk oxen are, and each year he takes me to at least one new, prime gathering locale, well off the beaten path—magical spots, where prize patches of qiviut await discovery, and the hulking beasts watch from the willows. At some point, Kevin wanted one hand-spun knit hat, a trophy, a living garment crafted from earth and beast, in exchange for handing over his pickings. We've gathered lots together over the years, and he's long since gotten his hat.

One day, long after moose season was over and autumn had faded to a gray, pre-winter chill, Kevin confessed to me: he killed a musk ox bull. I knew this day was coming, but I had put it out of my mind. I felt as though the musk ox belonged to me, a sacred beast, provider of exquisite fiber, my dream time familiar. Eating them just didn't seem right—hunting them even worse. He knew how I felt and yet got a permit to kill one long before he told me of his plans. We argued. Though we fill our freezer with wild meat and fish each year, I made declarations about not eating musk ox. No, I could not reconcile myself to it. I huffed and threw daggers with my eyes when he brought a leg in the house to butcher. I looked at the hide hanging on a pole outside, peeking now and then through the window, and watched him flesh it out. The hide, it seemed like the very essence of the creature.

I questioned myself. Wasn't I, after all, a spinster? Wasn't I a woman who sits in her house at the edge of the tundra and prays for bad weather so she can shut herself in and draw forth the thread of her destiny as she sees fit? I thought of the Three Fates that spin the thread, weave the thread into life's tapestry, then cut the thread at life's end. Is it so outrageous that we should kill and eat a musk ox, allow it to nourish us? I watched Kevin, who smelled of blood and grease, silently cut meat at our kitchen table. Expertly he separated flesh from bone, his back to me as he reduced the musk ox to its parts, so much less than the whole.

He tiptoed around me in the kitchen when cooking some musk ox for himself, aware of my hypersensitivity about the issue. He tempted me with tastes of steak and juicy burgers. Eventually my animal nature won and I tried some musk ox meat. Oh, it was good! Succulent, deliciously fatty, and moist. The hide returned from the tannery and was a wondrous thing to me with its deep pile and coarse guard hairs—some two feet long—that once brushed the tundra and swayed in the wind. Here was a completion in my relationship to this animal: fiber, food, spirit.

Kevin and I come down off the mountain at three a.m. from a midsummer-night hike. As we traipse back to the truck, my knees complain, but my spirit sings. We avoid a musk ox bull we saw on the way up. My pack is full of qiviut from this very bull, and I'm half hoping that on the way home I won't find any more. Our black-and-white border collie loses herself to bird chasing. The sky is aglow in twilight and the tundra luminescent, lit from within. A lone yellow-crowned sparrow whistles his three-note song.

Home the next day, I unfurl my gathering scarf, lay out the luscious hunks of qiviut. Smoky browns, a pale beige, the black coarseness of some guard hairs—this is a lot, this will keep me busy. I label this bag "Sunset Rock." I will reserve and spin from this qiviut one single skein. That one skein will become a hat, or a scarf, or a section of the shawl I'm planning. Thrilled by the possibilities, I can't resist. I pull the thread from a half-filled bobbin through the orifice and set the wheel to turning. As it spins I join the old thread with a new fluff, draw out my right hand and watch as fiber twists into yarn.

Wilderburb Burrows

PEGGY SHUMAKER

I step outside and shovel a path through the snow, to the intake of my log home's holding tank. Only ten inches of the stick come up wet. I'll have to drive eight miles to town, fill the tank in my pickup, drive back, hook up the fire hose, and set its nozzle into the pipe. Then I'll have to clamber back uphill and turn the valve, listening while water rushes down through the hose into the tank buried deep, too deep to freeze. When I invested in the hauling tank and hose, I called the Water Wagon man who'd been delivering—at six cents per gallon.

"I'll be hauling my own water," I told him, feeling strong and self-reliant.

"Okay," he said cheerfully. "See you in February."

He was right. In the days of darkness and deep cold, I don't want to handle anything wet, don't want to stand still outside even for a few minutes.

How can animals that don't migrate or hibernate bear it, being outside night and day? The cold's painful. Even with wool liners and double fleece mitts, my hands ache. The skin across my face tightens, threatens to break. Air passages ice up. Everything slows down—machinery, metabolisms, minds.

Once it's frozen around here, in mid-October say, it stays frozen until May. I use my back deck as extra freezer space, laying out shrink-wrapped fillets of salmon caught at Valdez and stashing bags of peas in a plastic bin.

I bury in the snow an extra turkey bought on sale. Around breakup, I'll try to finish the deck food, inviting friends to share what's thawing. But for now, the hard cold guards my stash.

After bones leave the soup kettle, I set out on the deck the remains of a chicken. The few shreds of meat disappear fast. Rendered fat scooped off cooled broth freezes in seconds and instantly draws in winged cannibals—ravens, camp robbers, and chickadees, black-capped and boreal. One pair of hairy woodpeckers hunkered down for the long haul stops by for a bite. Burly, the winter birds. How can they pass the word so quickly? Are they watching all the time? I cut one corner of the birdseed bag and lay out a windrow the length of the deck rail. The winged ones scatter as much as they eat, small cascades of plenty raining down for pikas and voles.

Two enterprising voles discover one small tube of summer; they gnaw and claw through the screen over the dryer vent and brave the secret passageway through the log wall. Axl, one of the Great Cats of the Universe, toys with them. He lets them putter, scouting the edges of their new world. Then he crouches, gathering all his power. Unleashed, he launches sky high, lands precisely so his paws surround a panicked nub of fur, nips it up by the tail and tosses it toward the rafters. Good thing for Axl there's no closed season, no bag limit, on voles.

The cat, a spoiled kid playing with his food, has no idea what it takes for tiny mammals to winter over. We humans don't know a whole lot more. We've observed that voles like to snuggle up during the cold months, seven or so to a burrow. Close company in communal nests—one way to stay warm. A winter of seven-vole nights causes them to lose body mass and grow thicker fur. They share cached food and defend together against predators and thieves. They carve intricate tunnels under the snow. I love picturing the life I do not see. Those blue-tinged corridors, subsurface territories warmed by the earth and insulated by snow. Down there, the temperature stays about thirty-two degrees Fahrenheit, no matter how frigid the air above the snow pack. Within their tunnels and burrows, voles move around on the coldest nights. And they've developed internal chemical reactions that warm them up—vole hot flashes.

But warmth isn't the only variable. One decades-long study shows that survival of tundra and taiga voles depends on the abundance of dwarf-shrub berries they store over the summer. In other places, voles depend on small roots, fungi, lichens, and grasses. The number of voles determines in large part the populations of all the animals they feed—owls, weasels, foxes, lynx, and wolves. In some places, even waking bears dig for them, clawing up pawfuls of scrambling fur.

Mostly I see only their tracks, ditto marks skittering across fresh snow. Sometimes in late summer I see the grass mounds, the bundles tiny rodents stash at strategic locations. Voles and pika stay awake all year, tunneling under snow to their burrows and hoards, surfacing once in a while. Do they long, as I do, for a glimpse of the sun? Just a reminder—a reassurance—that the sun we count on will, in fact, rise one day? They must—vole reproduction is linked to sunlight. Right now the winter sun barely makes an appearance, limps along the horizon for a couple of hours, then ducks back out of sight.

How can they stand it, animals that survive thirty, forty, fifty below? Ravens commute, forty miles sometimes, to play in the updrafts at the university's power plant. They gorge themselves at the Pizza Hut dumpster, then take off before dusk and return to nests hidden where nobody walking can follow.

Interior Alaska is a place too cold for roaches or fleas—they don't survive their first winter. It's a place where some trees, with a blast loud as cannon shot, crack up. Canvasbacks, buffleheads, Arctic terns, Canada geese, and snow geese pass right on through. They nest up north, then bring their young to bulk up on barley spread at Creamer's Field before they fly. Some feel the pull as far south as Tierra del Fuego. Sandhill cranes open themselves fully, wings wide, legs stretched, as they float down onto the field. They wander, jabber, flutter, scold. They keep to their families, attentive to their young for one last journey. Some tangle, but settle things without touching, their red crowns slashing the meadow. I revel in their angular flapping dance. Gawky on land, they lift off, Lincolnesque, into the blue.

On this earth, under it, Arctic ground squirrels gear up for the dark time. All summer, squirrels munch everything in sight. I've seen them chow down on grasses, buds, leaves, stems, roots. I've watched spruce squirrels devour bugs, cat food, overripe pears, peanut butter, birdseed. Once a ruddy pair snacked on the carcass of a chickadee that flew headfirst into the pane.

They fatten up and slow down. During eight months of hibernation, ground squirrels curl up two feet under the tundra. The squirrel's heart, kidney, and liver rest at below-freezing temperatures for weeks at a time. Brian Barnes, a scientist who plants sensors inside squirrels, has been figuring out exactly how this happens, what processes allow them to survive, revive, thrive. They're the only mammals that can supercool. In a lab, their blood would crystallize. But inside the squirrels, blood courses, liquid at twenty-seven degrees Fahrenheit. Perhaps one day we can imitate part of this in astronauts or surgical patients. One day, we might be able to prolong the shelf life of human organs for transplant. But for the moment, we're intrigued by these efficient mysteries.

All summer, squirrels' loud chatter—the staccato CHK-CHK-CHK-CHK-CHK-CHK—lets me know I'm not alone. They're pretty sure they have little to fear, and they'll run right up to any stranger, baring their teeth. But when they do get worried, they flatten themselves along the duff or tundra and bolt for the safety of their burrows.

One August the choppy voices grow louder. Above my bed, furtive rustlings. I don't think much about it. Next night, more scratching, closer. What's on the roof? I go outside, but even in bright moonlight, don't see a thing. I hear them, whatever they are, nearer now. The third night, a wild chase scene erupts, a rumble. Right over my head. Just waking, I begin to think, *squirrels*. Drowsy, I realize the squirrels aren't *on* the roof. They're under it, somewhere between the shingles and the ceiling.

I'd like to live peacefully with my neighbors. But the changes they're making could cut off my furnace, my lights. I can hear them ripping insulation, yanking on wiring. Nesting.

Usually, I'm fine out here. But it can unnerve some people, just being in the woods. One visiting writer, invited to use the house while I was away, had to turn around and retreat to a motel room in town. She was just too much a city person to live even a few days where there were more trees than people. She was terrified of seeing a moose. Why do we sigh, once we've eluded some danger, real or imagined, that we're "out of the woods"?

Maybe I don't have the good sense to be afraid when I should. I've never seen bears out here. But a pile of dried scat, stuffed with blueberries and small bones, gives me a thrill—just to know that a wild one has been so close. I never sensed it, never knew. And all those clusters of tawny oblong pellets—moose have drawn near, more often than I realized, conducting their own lives for their own reasons. I only found out later. These squirrels, though, could do big damage, damage I don't know how to fix myself.

My niece, away from home for the first time, loads her cheap pellet rifle. A joke. She's been practicing on homemade targets, hitting mostly the ground around the cardboard. She lifts the barrel, puts her eye to the sight, lines up, aiming for a squirrel sniffing upright on the woodshed roof. Pa-ching! She nails him as if he were a metal silhouette in a shooting gallery. Stunned, she bursts into tears. She feels so badly we have a funeral. While I bury the carcass in a small circle of birch, she sobs.

How should we evict the ones rollicking overhead? I research Havahart traps, thinking that after all, I'm living in their forest and they're only trying to find a decent place to winter. A friend tells me how completely territorial Arctic squirrels are. If one gets on somebody else's turf, the established squirrels will kill the intruder or run him off into some other squirrels' territory. So with no delusions of compassion, I close off every entry place but one and set out rattraps. The next morning I climb the ladder two stories and check the trap under the gambrel roof. It sickens me to find a camp robber, limp, snapped by the metal bar.

Then a friend has a great idea—an escape chute, one way. A slide the whole family can enjoy. We rig up a length of aluminum dryer vent. We unscrew one of the recessed canister lights and push the vent up inside the deck's eave. Duct tape to the rescue—we secure it. This offers the squirrels a way out. They'll get hungry before long, or will have the instinct to cache more food near this nest. The tube's sides are too smooth to let them climb back up. At least, I hope so.

Over the next four days, I watch for them. One tries to wedge itself in the slick tube, but can't gain purchase. She thumps onto the deck. The rest slip down and thud, then shake their heads and zip into the trees.

After this, they help themselves at the deck rail, chittering at the cat going crazy behind the glass. From my small pocket of warmth, I take heart, watching. They don't even look up when I pass by.

Things That Go Bump

NED ROZELL

Rain falls at 10:38 p.m., and the glow of a candle next to me is the only light for many square miles. I am alone in a plywood cabin, waiting for a noise in the night.

I'm as scared as a boy alone in a tent for the first time, and I can't believe my luck. The hunting guide I work for has left me on a lonely stretch of a river that empties into the Yukon. A moose-hunting client canceled his hunt because of heart trouble, so my boss, Len, decided to leave me alone at the little green cabin while he returned to his other hunters at a larger camp downriver. He said he would return with the next client in eight days.

"You can scout the area for moose," he said. "Use the canoe to get a feel for the country."

Employed as a packer, I have for the last month carried the meat of sheep and moose shot by men from outside Alaska who have paid thousands of dollars for the privilege. I have cooked for them, carried their gear, and listened to stories of animals they have killed.

I've had my fill of hunting stories. Now, much of the time, I prefer solitude to company. I was ecstatic with the promise of eight days by myself in the wild.

Len's Super Cub rattled west over hills of birch and muskeg early this morning. In the wake of the plane, I felt a silence so powerful I opened my mouth to quiet my breathing, savoring the gurgle of the river.

I'm not the only mammal in this large green-and-brown patch of Alaska. A grizzly bear shares my space. Yesterday, before Len left me at the cabin, we repaired a hole the bear had torn in the plywood wall. The hole was as large as a basketball hoop. Once the bear chewed and clawed its way through layers of glued wood, it sampled everything inside, coating the floor with cooking oil and other hard-to-remove ingredients. To patch the hole, we tacked a square of plywood spiked with nails like a porcupine.

I met the cabin invader this afternoon. I was floating the river in the canoe, tossing a Pixie at a slough in hopes of a pike dinner. I saw movement on a willow-and-spruce hillside and picked up my binoculars.

The grizzly was running uphill with good speed, blond and beautiful, shoulders rippling. I drifted close to a riverbank that filled the binoculars with willows, and I lost the bear. I made a note to tell Len on our ten p.m. radio check.

The river arced to the north to where a gravel bar and cutbank pinched the brown water to a mere five yards across. As I rounded a bend, the bear was there at the squeeze, hunkered on the gravel bar. With the fluid motion of a panther, he paced toward the approaching canoe.

The riverbank crumbled beneath his heavy steps. He stumbled, but kept advancing, closing the distance between us to fifty yards.

I thought of the large-caliber rifle tied to the middle seat of the canoe, out of reach. I looked at the round face of the bear, which crashed along the riverbank, sniffing the air as though his nose could pull me toward him.

I yanked the starter cord of the canoe's motor. The blessed Honda fired and fell into idle. I shifted to reverse, thinking I could back away from him, but the canoe stood in place against the current, and water spilled over the square stern. I clunked the motor out of reverse and into forward, turning the canoe upstream in a wide arc, feeling the jerk of current when the canoe turned broadside.

Then I was motoring upstream in a seventeen-foot canoe, losing a race to a bear galloping through cottongrass like a thoroughbred. Twisting the throttle, I looked to my left and watched the bear, all rolling muscle and determination, with just five yards of muddy water between us. He chased me upstream as he would a moose calf, and I wondered what I would do if he jumped in the water and torpedoed me.

He tore along the bank, pausing once to stand and sniff the air. For a few seconds, I felt the terror and exhilaration of a hunted animal.

As the bear and I raced upstream like a greyhound and a mechanical bunny, we came to a wide spot where a slough oozed into the river. The bear chose to go around the slough rather than swim across, giving me a welcome buffer of forty yards. I U-turned the canoe, holding my breath as the current whipped the bow downstream.

The bear stood, its front paws dropping at its side. My eight-horsepower motor and the seven-mile-per-hour push of the river were too much. I pulled away, looking back at the brown spot that disappeared as I rounded a bend.

The cabin was three miles downstream of the bear. As soon as I reached the familiar mud bar, I beached the canoe and reached for my .338 Magnum, untying the loop of parachute cord that fastened it to the canoe. The gun was in my hands until I stepped inside the dark little cabin.

After making dinner, I called Len on the two-way radio. A commander of men in Vietnam, Len knew what it felt like to be hunted by his own species, and he had once killed a bear that was rushing to kill him. He gave me advice to sleep on.

"If he starts ripping through that door, you just blow his shit away," Len said. "I have no problem with that."

With that, we said goodnight. I clicked off the radio, its hiss dying a few seconds later. My ears tuned to the silence. Intermittent drops of rain on the metal roof sped my heart a few beats.

In the privileged world in which I live, there's not much to fear. No one is trying to kill me; I can survive with my senses at half power. This bear probably does not want to kill me, but I know he's stronger than me, faster than me, and he can detect my presence long before I can his. What did he want out there? Did he think I was a swimming moose, about to stumble through wet mud onto his side of the river? Did my scent remind him of the maple syrup he sampled at the cabin?

The bear has ground the dull edge off my senses. I can't shake the image of his round, determined face, of his eyes locked on the canoe, of teeth and claws ripping through plywood.

My fear is ridiculous. I could drop an elephant with the rifle leaning next to me. If Len were with me, I would not be scared at all. Being alone strips me of everything but me. I'm left with the wide eyes of a seven-year-old trying to make sense of a night animal's shriek.

I set a flashlight by the bunk, its bulb pointing toward the door. I rehearse a mental routine—switch on the light, click off the safety, point the gun at the hole being ripped in the door, fire. Paranoid, for sure, but I can think of nothing else.

I light a candle. Its soft light shines through the south window of the cabin, touching the gnarled willows outside. I am alone in the middle of Alaska, waiting for a noise in the night.

Sleeping with Otters

JENNIFER HAHN

As I paddled up the north shore of Seaforth Channel, the islands seemed to be raising their walls. I'd seen only three possible campsites all afternoon. A new spot looked promising, but, eyeing the forest that lay behind a mattress-size beach of broken shells, I was again disheartened. Telltale kelp fronds hung like Christmas garlands from the trees' lowest branches. By midnight this lovely pocket beach would be an aquarium.

At least the spring sun is on my side, I told myself. In these northern latitudes gauzy light can linger in the sky long after sundown. The crepuscular hours, the hours before night swallows the last light, were among my favorites to paddle. On the Inside Passage, the sea was often calmer then. And shy animals—both nocturnal and diurnal—pawed about their business in the wide open. But that night, traveling alone and without a secure camp, twilight was a gloomy and worrisome time.

Due west, where Seaforth Channel surged into Milbanke Sound, the Inside Passage makes a dogleg turn north and winds through hundreds of miles of unseen fjords. Staring down Seaforth toward Milbanke Sound, miles before I'd take that northward turn, I saw only sky and sea. Both appeared the color of skim milk. The horizon was erased. Reflection and reflected melted into one monochromatic canvas from hull to zenith. I had no reference point to aim the bow at. Paddling through this waterscape, hanging weightless as a dream, the winged kayak rode somewhere between two worlds. Such a calm, reflective sea can be dangerous. In a matter of minutes, I nearly dozed off with the paddle loosely gripped.

If it weren't for a southbound prawn boat that suddenly emerged from a hard-to-see passage a quarter mile ahead, my next landmark for pointing north would have remained hidden. Paddle-sore from fourteen continuous hours of progress and lacking sleep, it was time for me to prop the paddle up against a tree. I was so tired that I would have missed the otter family altogether if it hadn't been for a curious sneezing sound—*Stissk! Stissk!*—emerging from an offshore kelp bed.

Five feet away, two almond-shaped heads the color of wet cedar bark corked up. The otters blinked at me. I looked wide eyed at them. We all three seemed to say, "Where'd YOU come from?"

Their broad foreheads were chiseled down the center with a perfect part. Stiff whiskers punctuated their brows and curved neatly back from their alert noses. Called vibrissae, these extra-sensory receptors actually vibrate against rocks, fish, crabs, and kelp. They tell the otter what is good pickin's—especially in murky water.

Drifting in silhouette, the otters' humped backs and whip tails appeared serpentine. The shape shouted: river otters! Suddenly the larger otter rushed toward me, raising its furred snout skyward to snag a scent of my who-abouts.

Lutra (otter) *canadensis* (since it was first described in Canada) *pacifica* (because this frolicsome clan adores Pacific coastal waterways) is the species' scientific name. River otter is the common name, but "river" is a misnomer in coastal places and a culprit of confusion because it leads to innumerable mistaken identities of *Lutra canadensis* as a sea otter.

It's easy to understand the confusion. In the Pacific Northwest, river otters, like sea otters, make their living by the ocean. Dining on crabs, spiny sculpins, gunnel fish, snails, and a favorite delicacy, pinto abalone, river otters, alongside the mink and fisher (a relative of the marten), have evolved to be among the most skilled ocean hunters. A difference between the two otter types is that river otters don't raft up for the night. They galumph ashore. Sea otters (*Hydra lutras*), on the other hand, spend their lives waterborne—including nighttime, when they spool their shoulders, pups, and flippered hind feet in a golden cradle of kelp leaves and float, belly to the stars.

Tragically, the sea otter's snuggly, waterproof fur nearly led to its demise. In the early nineteenth century fur traders poured into the Bella Bella territory in search of valuable otter pelts, stopping at Milbanke Sound to trade. Quick to capitalize on the profits, the Hudson Bay Company tacked up a trading post on Campbell Island. Within decades, British Columbia's and Washington's sea otters were bludgeoned off the face of the coast. Today, new rafts of sea otters have been reintroduced from Alaska. River otters, however, still thrive in their original range along wild stretches of the protected Inside Passage.

People are still an otter's biggest enemy. Around the world, populations of all twelve species of otters are plummeting through loss of habitat and profit-driven killing by humans. In western Canada alone, trappers kill up to five thousand five hundred yearly for their soft pelts. In the wilds, great horned owls, eagles, and large fish snag unwary kits. Bobcats, lynx, wolves, and coyotes stalk otters as they trot between lakes, streams, and their denlike homes.

You can catch a whiff of a river otter's home when you are sea kayaking downwind, even as far away as a quarter mile! The musky smell is unmistakable. Otters are in the family Mustelid, as are the notoriously aromatic skunk and the mink, weasel, badger, and marten.

A pair of scent glands hides under a Mustelid member's tail. To flag territory, river otters drag their tails over driftwood, tree branches, and low-slung ferns. They even gather armfuls of leaves and rub them like handkerchiefs over belly, crotch, and back. They also dribble urine on vegetation. The lingering bouquet serves as an olfactory billboard for sexual receptivity. It clues in kin as to how much time has elapsed since the last swabbing. Rabble-rousing otter families can cloak a favorite islet or peninsula with a distinct composite of scents. Long before a kayaker steps ashore to relieve herself, the woods are as odoriferous as a latrine.

In 1983, when I first kayaked through the Inside Passage with Gene Meyers, we stumbled upon otter terrain while searching for a level tent site. I learned to recognize small plots denuded of plants and tamped down to fine flour as otter rolling patches. Flat and wide enough to erect a two-person tent, they became our last-ditch answer for lodging. Often on the go, otters hunker down at one spot for just a few days at a time. Adults move about within a home range of up to sixty miles, revisiting fishing spots, dens, promontories, and rolling patches. Since it was dusk, and I had no camp, I figured it was okay to take temporary shelter in an otter home if no other was available. With a little luck, these streamlined swimmers would lead me to such a swatch amid these towering island shores.

With a good frog kick, the largest otter, probably a male, buoyed its square shoulders and chest completely out of the water. He was four and a half feet long, sleek as a comma, and one-third tail. His chin bore a silver sheen like reflected moonlight. We locked eyes. What was he thinking? His russet fur glistened with the sea. Uncertain of the danger, he snuffed the air repeatedly. Wavering back and forth cobra style, he seemed to be triangulating my body size and distance.

Four feet behind me another noise erupted. It sounded like water spewed from a swimmer's snorkel. *Piff! Piff! Piff!* Six more otters popped up. Smaller than the first two, these were undoubtedly the kits. They appeared more nervous, turning heads quickly side to side, eyeing each other, watching their parents, eyeing me. Except for craning my neck, I floated still as a drift log.

The father, after giving me a thorough once-over, dropped back to the waterline satisfied. He executed a graceful U-turn and flowed back to the clan, tail trailing behind.

Six kits are about the biggest brood a river otter can muster. Two or three are more common. The wonderful thing is that river otters, like their sea otter sisters, have a choice about when to deliver. Due to nature's trick of delayed implantation for in utero eggs, a mother can give birth as much as a year after mating. Yet, embryos mature in two months. It's a fascinating option for otter family planning. When fishing is grim, wait until spring.

These curious fishers were likely born in late winter. When I packed for this trip, they had been naked, blind, and squirming about in their den, or holt.

Within a second of the parents' return, the family formed a tight-moving cluster. Swimming off, heads pumping in perfect unison, they followed their internal compasses west. The otters aimed for a jawbone of islands on the light-flooded horizon that I hadn't seen until now. Having nowhere else to go, I followed the eight distinct wakes.

Virtuoso swimmers, the shy otters soon outdistanced me. Four webbed paws and a long tail rudder give them great advantage over minks, weasels, and single kayaks. When hurried, otters tuck stubbly legs out of harm's way and propel forward by flexing up and down in a continuous wave from head to tail tip. In this fishlike fashion, they can attain speeds of almost seven miles per hour.

In my heart's prayer, I hoped for an island beach I could camp on for one to three days. Thanks to the otters, an hour before Milbanke Sound, an islet unfolded like a dream. It was ear-shaped with a pocket beach on the leeward side, crowned in spruce and cedar and skirted by a garden of wing kelp. It looked fifty yards wide at most.

The song of a Swainson's thrush rose from an invisible balcony in the greenery. Something splashed. I turned and discovered a seal escorting me shoreward. Without having to lift the paddle, I was carried forward by a tidal current filling the islet's bay. I simply ruddered with the blade to dodge rocks.

After anchoring the kayak leash behind three slippery rocks, I pulled myself up and onto a large drift log for easier walking. Where the bark shucked off, the wood looked as lustrous as abalone. Like an elevated walkway, the log stretched seventy feet up the beach onto a peninsula where it had heaved loose. I followed its steeply angled trunk to a tangled root mass and climbed down to the hidden pocket where the roots had grown. Standing beside the eight-foot-wide bowl, I was delighted that I could see deep into the wooded island.

I eagerly scouted for a tent site. Yet leather-leaf salal bushes barricaded the island's center as far as I could see. Every few feet a spruce trunk rose up, bearded with lichen. I didn't want to crash through and tear up an island. So without attempting to bushwhack any farther, I imagined my tent squeezed into this one lumpy but fortuitously clear spot. Otter signs lay scattered every which way around my sandaled feet. Husks of red rock crab claws had been sucked empty and light as a thimble. Silver ears of abalone were scooped clean. There were shards of mica-thin fish scales, toothpick ribs, vertebrae cemented in a column, and an arrowhead fish tail. Crouching down to lift up the treasures, I accidentally caught sight of a passage into the salal. Was this a portal to somewhere else? What, I wondered, lay on the other side?

Without hesitating, I dropped on my knees and crawled through an arch meant for an otter's shoulders. Branches caught my hair, hooked my sunglasses' cord, and thwacked my rib bones. I recalled the tale of Alice tumbling down the rabbit hole—except I landed in a bed of ginger-speckled chocolate lilies. Pollen the color of cornmeal brushed my shoulders. Where the lilies ended, a fallen tree arrowed off into the thick forest. I stood upright and walked across it like a bridge over a ravine. It led to another passage, this time framed with scarlet huckleberries.

On this one-acre secluded island, I bumped into otter signs without much trying. Scat, piled in neat thumb-thick rolls colored pink by crab-shell confetti, crackled under my knees. A tamped-down, tunnel-like trail scampered off under an umbrella of huckleberry, salal, and devil's club. No wider than a car tire, the serpentine path wound up and over fallen branches, through and around a cedar's leviathan roots, leading me to circumnavigate the island's perimeter. It took about twenty minutes.

With my greenhorn tracking skills, I soon lost the otter trail. The next scat I came to—on a boulder overlooking the sea—was greasy black and littered with shards of fish bone and insect chitin. I realized I was now tracking a weasel or a mink. But as serendipity would have it, I found something else imminently more useful. Towering above that greasy boulder was a great cedar tree. It beckoned me.

I climbed the small cliff to its trunk and found the holy grail of that evening's search—a near-level tent spot. I returned to the kayak, shuttled armfuls of gear up and down the cliff, and pitched my tent under a shelter of fragrant boughs. Lying in the tent that first night, I had the unmistakable sensation of roots pressing up against the tent floor. I unzipped the nylon door, lifted up the tent, and dug out two moon snail shells large as duck eggs and covered in moss—likely deposited by otters years ago.

Henry and Julia Speck, a Kwakiutl family I stayed with on Hope Island in 1983, called the land otter "*xomda.*" They pronounced the word as if they were imitating the sound of a revving motorcycle engine: *HOghh-mm-dah.* The name mimicked the otter's fluttering, throaty call.

Otters are chatterers. They whistle and grunt. They talk among themselves in a repertoire of voices. To contact kin, otters emit a terse, one-syllable *chirp!* When threatened or alarmed they growl like a dog. Inquiring, they seem to utter, *hah?* Parents talk with each other and the kits in a singsong, staccato chuckle. It's a sound I've learned to imitate by vibrating the back of my throat while exhaling. I can raise or lower the tone by pursing my lips.

I awoke in the sun-dappled tent to something wheezing, followed by a choking cough. "Otter!" I gasped. Maybe with an ill-lodged fish bone? Ducking behind the cedar trunk, I scanned the low-tide beach. Beyond the screen of cedar boughs, below the cliff, a female otter rooted through a mass of kelp. Behind her, two kits sinuous as wrestlers in furry leotards rough-and-tumbled on the beach. Shell bits flew. Growls and excited *whoffs* were exchanged in the combat. Muscular tails swung out and circled back for added balance. Their copper fur had a mussy look, like they'd just rolled out of the shower. I was thrilled at my good fortune and rifled the tent for binoculars.

I located the father otter fishing in a rocky tide pool. In a matter of seconds he surfaced with a wiggly gunnel fish. Holding the eel-shaped, olive-colored gunnel between his spread forepaws and a rock, he tore off chunks with sharp white canines. His dripping back hunched against the blue sea.

When it comes to food, otters are not cuddly. They are feisty hunters with a carnivorous sweet tooth. Like cormorants and loons, otters float along the water's surface, head down, trolling with shifting eyes. Stealthy as submarines, otters can ambush swimming water birds, but they prefer to dine on crabs, fish, chitons, urchins, frogs, and shellfish. If desperate, they have been known to stalk right into the lodge of a muskrat or beaver and knock them dead.

On land, these intelligent hunters ambush rodents and rabbits. Some manage to steal away with a couple of bird's eggs or even a bird. Come winter, otters dive through holes in lake ice and hurl crappies and bluegills up through the opening to crunch on later. Some have punched holes through beaver dams, waited for the water to pour off, and then waded in to munch up marooned fish and frogs.

For a long time, I sat with binoculars held in one hand and a notebook in the other. The father and mother otter were hunting. Working together, they herded spiny sculpin fish into the shallows, where the waiting kits gobbled them with gusto. Once the female dug her paws into the mud to excavate a huge moon snail. The youngsters pitched in, digging alongside.

An eagle whistled overhead. Both parents scanned the air and growled to alert the kits. Otters may not be graceful on land, but they surely are swift. Alarmed, they can gallop faster than a human—but not as fast as an eagle flies. The mother sprinted toward the kits—springing forward, humping furry spine, grazing forepaws with the back pair. Within seconds she was forty yards up the beach, corralling the kits up a bank. They whined and scrabbled, barely reaching a thicket of salal. The eagle passed low over the beach as if there were no commotion at all.

Not wanting to lose sight of this family, I crawled back down the cliff. Like a kid playing cops and robbers, I snuck along the island's edge, ducking behind giant beach logs and boulders. I worked halfway around the island before spying the mother and kits.

They lounged and groomed outside a hidey-hole near a tangle of cedar roots. Out beyond the kelp line in the wind-pleated water, the father continued to fish. His tail snapped spray with each dunk and dive. Fathers rejoin the family after the kits reach six months to help teach the youngsters how to become self-sufficient little fishers and hunters. I lay belly down on a beach log watching through a peekaboo hole in a log's root mass, utterly enchanted. Seeing these wild creatures—undisturbed, safe—was the antidote to my frightful experiences in civilization. I'd come here to find peace. Watching the otters was the ideal activity for just that.

I spent two days playing otter hide-and-seek. One night, in the pitch dark, something leapt twice on the tent as if it were a trampoline; I guessed it was my otter friends, as I discovered a freshly scoured abalone shell outside in the morning. From underneath the cedar tree I watched the two kits ferry driftwood back and forth on their noses like one yards a ball down a lawn in field hockey. They also played tug-of-war with what appeared to be a giant gumboot chiton.

Later, bathing in the shallows and scrubbing my messy face with a seaweed leaf, I felt a host of prickly chin hairs sprouting. I didn't care. I liked the evolution. Why bother to tweeze anything? Taking up handfuls of gritty sand, I scrubbed arms, legs, pits, and shoulders. I noticed the fur on my legs was longer and blond from the sun. Lacking aromatic soap, my scent was muskier. Maybe being a hairy, stinky sort of gal would dub me less attractive to any man with harmful intentions. The island was dousing me with its magic. I was growing a new kind of skin.

The Circle of the Kill

NICK JANS

I was sixty miles from home when I saw the tracks—those of a lone moose, nothing special except that they were fresh, crisply etched in new snow, and headed in the same direction I was. Tired from five days of traveling with a heavy sled, I watched them disappear under my snowmobile's skis without paying much notice. I'd already come seventy miles from the northern rim of the Noatak valley, across the Imelyak, and over the rolling high tundra of Amakomanaq—an unmarked trail Clarence had shown me years ago. Ahead lay Ivishak Pass, a notorious wind tunnel, and I wanted to get through while the morning calm held.

Another set of tracks merged in from the left. Wolf. I slowed down, leaned forward, and started paying attention. The size of the prints meant a young adult or a big pup, and here and there the loping animal's paws blurred over the moose trail. Then other wolves joined in from the east, more tracks than I could sort out. The snow before me was trampled in a maze, and there was a mound of wolf scat. Probably a day or two old, I thought, and slowed down for a look. Where was the pack now? I skidded to a stop. The pile was steaming. For the first time in a quarter mile I looked up, and fifty yards away a wolf stood in the ice fog. Tail out, stiff-legged, it regarded me, and our eyes met.

Something in the stare of a wolf is chilling, beyond the hungry yellow eyes of childhood nightmares, beyond any physical threat, real or imagined.

Caught in that cold glare, I felt suddenly transparent, as if my heart were being measured. In that instant I knew what we fear most in wolves: not their teeth but their wisdom—an alien, elusive intelligence that refuses us, rejecting our notions of superiority with a glance.

We faced each other, motionless in the half-light, suspended in our surprise. I watched the pulsing steam of its breath, and realized I'd been holding mine. Then the wolf turned. Things began to move again. I followed its gaze to a nearby slope, and there were dark shapes in the brush, a dozen wolves standing together, looking down toward us, waiting for what would happen next. Ravens rose and circled, squawking. The wolf in my trail stepped toward me and stopped. The next move was mine.

In thirteen years of moving through wolf country, I've felt menaced only once, and that animal, young and inexperienced, probably meant no harm. Every wolf I've ever encountered—maybe four dozen in all that time—has either turned tail or ignored me. Here, riding a snowmobile and carrying a rifle, I knew there was no danger. In fact, I was surprised that the wolves had allowed themselves to be seen. Even in these remote mountains, hundreds of miles from the nearest road, most packs have learned that snowmobiles mean trouble—Eskimo wolf hunters, my friends among them. Why, then, was this wolf not only standing its ground, but approaching?

Maybe he was speaking to me. The wolf stepped toward me and stopped. I eased my idling machine forward an equal distance. The wolf repeated his question, and I answered again. There was surely no threat between us now, only curiosity, a desire to know. Forty yards apart, we studied each other. I don't know what the wolf saw. I remember a long-legged, thin, silver gray creature with a shabby coat and luminous eyes, head down, ears cocked, probing, poised on the edge of motion.

Then he was gone. In a blur I felt more than saw, the wolf pivoted and launched himself uphill in an explosion of sinewed grace. Ahead, the pack was in full flight, heads out, tails back, merging into single file as they burst up the slope, running hard for a windswept crag far above the valley floor. Pausing on the skyline, they took a last look and disappeared.

Halfway up the slope I found the kill. Entrails, bones, clumps of hair, and bloody snow were all that remained of the moose. Even the hide had been gnawed and swallowed, and bones cracked for their thread of marrow. The skull, still attached to the spine, had been polished clean. The story of the hunt was there in the snow: The cow had been trotting along the base of the ridge when the first wolf appeared behind her. She turned several times, harassed but not seriously threatened. Distracted, she sensed the ambush too late. The wolves charged downhill through the brush. She wheeled, but was driven back by the first wolf. The pack surrounded her and drew blood, slashing at flanks and hindquarters. More wolves arrived. While some rested, others pressed home the attack. The snow was trampled in circular patterns over several hundred yards, and at each place the cow had made a stand.

Finally, she floundered uphill into deep snow. The wolves pursued, and one slashed in, splitting open her belly. She struggled another thirty yards, dragging her entrails. The end came quickly as the pack mobbed her off her feet.

By the time I'd arrived, no more than three hours later, she had almost disappeared. Thirteen wolves had eaten over six hundred pounds of flesh—close to fifty pounds each. Nearby was a place where the pack had sat together, and I imagined them full bellied, heads tilted back, singing of the hunt.

I spent more than an hour near the kill, circling as the wolves had done, reading their story in the snow, studying spots of blood, bits of hair. The intertwined trails seemed graceful, as if the wolves and moose had danced together. At the end of their dance lay the kill, beautiful in its simplicity. There was no horror on this silent white hillside. This was their life—an endless hunt, an endless celebration of death.

As I stood within the circle of the kill, looking down at wolf prints frozen in blood, I brushed against their secret: wolves understand death perfectly. That's the bright, cold wisdom we see in their eyes, the thing that makes us afraid. Death is their art, their beauty, while it's our darkness and terror. If we ever understood what they know, we've since forgotten. Maybe we're drawn to them because they remember.

The Porcupine Wars

DEBRA MCKINNEY

We were standing in the drizzle, watching a kayak race down Eagle River, when through the rowdiest stretch of rapids came this big brown blob.

Errant hairpiece?

Whatever it was, it slid over the first set of waves, got sucked under then spat back out, bounced off a rock, then bounced off another. As this thing pinballed downriver, it got closer and closer, until we could see it was some kind of animal.

Butt, snout, butt, snout.

At the bottom of the run, it bobbed a few seconds, then turned and started dog-paddling toward shore.

"Is that . . . a . . . porcupine?"

Porcupines may be pigeon-toed and bowlegged, with all the streamline features of a chimney brush, but they're known to be good swimmers. Those quills are hollow. And sporting something like thirty thousand of them makes these guys as buoyant as tub toys.

But crashing a Class III whitewater race?

Dumb.

The half-drowned porky paddled up, planted its front paws on solid ground and dragged its hindquarters ashore just a few feet away. If it noticed us, it didn't care. It stood there weaving awhile, shook itself, nearly tumbled over, and then, as if powered by tequila shooters, staggered off into the woods.

That was the first porcupine I'd ever seen. Knowing now what I didn't know then, I wish it had been my last.

Nothing personal.

I'm actually rather fond of the galoots, despite all the bad porcupine juju that's come our way since that first encounter, and despite the long and financially draining relationship we've had with Alaska's second largest rodent—the one with bad hair and no discernible neck.

We were living in Teller, a small Inupiaq village northwest of Nome, when porcupines started perforating our lives on a regular basis. Returning from an overnighter at an old mining camp, we were hiking along the tundra and were just about home when our dog, Eva, disappeared. We called and called. We backtracked and called some more. Then we heard yipping.

Half black lab, half St. Bernard, this dog had a head the size of a wrecking ball and was not the yipping type. When we finally found her down in a shallow gully, she looked more scrub brush than dog. Uzi-ed in the face by a porcupine, she had quills poking from her nose, jowls, lips, jaw, gums, tongue.

She pawed her face and shook her head violently, rattling the quills, driving them only deeper. Her bottom lip was so thickly spiked, it was stretched out of shape, her tongue so skewered, it no longer fit in her mouth.

One look at her and I dropped to my knees.

I thought of our Fairbanks friends who spend five months a year running a trap line way up in the Porcupine River country. When one of their sled dogs got nailed, they poured whiskey down her throat, hoping she'd pass out so they could get at the quills inside her mouth. But the dog could drink like a sailor. So they shot her up with Percodan. Still the pain was too much and she fought all their good intentions.

They could see it was hopeless. It was three hundred river miles to the road that dead-ends on the opposite side of the Yukon, then another one hundred and thirty of mostly gravel to reach the nearest vet. Rather than let her starve to death, they led her away from the dog yard, aimed the .357 and pulled the trigger.

We were much less prepared. Teller is a "dry" village, so we didn't even have so much as a can of Oly.

First we had to get Eva home, and she didn't want to budge. We led her awkwardly by the collar, and as we drew near the edge of town, a couple village kids saw us and came trotting over. Then a couple more. And a couple more.

"What's wrong with that dog?" asked a young girl. "She looks funny."

"Porcupine," I said. "She's hurt."

"I go get that porcupine," a boy offered, his eyes narrowing.

"Naw," I told him. "It was just trying to protect itself."

"I go get that porcupine," he said.

Just a few days before, one of the older boys had dropped a dead porcupine off on our doorstep—a goodwill offering to my husband, a new high school teacher in town. The boy had shot it and had heard Paul liked the meat.

Not really. He just hates to see anything go to waste. Particularly anything that could be put to good use on his dinner plate.

Earlier that fall, he'd come across a hunter from nearby Brevig Mission who'd killed a porcupine, cut off its feet and was leaving the rest. So Paul threw it in the boat, took it home, and salvaged the meat.

Butchering it outside drew quite a bit of interest. In Teller, people obviously eat all kinds of wild meat—musk ox, bearded seal, fermented fish heads, etc. But not porcupine. One bite and I understood why. To me, it tasted like a cross between duck and an oil change.

Once we got Eva home, we dropped our packs and called the village health aide, then walked to the edge of town to see Joe Garnie, an Iditarod musher and the wisest dog person we knew. Both offered condolences and antibiotics, but no secret home remedy for de-quilling a dog. Back at our place, we dug a pair of needle-nose pliers out of the toolbox and got to it.

If we'd known what we were in for, we wouldn't have bothered.

As if impalement weren't enough, porcupine quills are barbed with microscopic shingles that drive them deeper with each muscle contraction. Think fishhooks on the go. A broken-off or missed quill can go on a walkabout until it pierces an eye, a lung, or the heart.

At least one person has suffered death by porcupine. According to a 1958 report in the *New England Journal of Medicine*, the man swallowed a quill while eating a porcupine sandwich, and it took a tour of his innards, stabbing him from the inside out.

Unlike those of a cactus, the painful parts of a porcupine aren't a constant menace. Quills lie flat until called upon. When a porcupine feels threatened, its quills rise to attention, accompanied by the gnashing of teeth. If that doesn't get the message across, it turns its back, reverses engines, and swings its tail like a medieval mace.

Those quills hook in deep, which explains why Eva fought us like a wounded wolverine. She wouldn't let us near them. So we ended up making her a straitjacket out of duct tape by binding her front and back legs together. And because she'd jerk away when she saw pliers descending, we blindfolded her by taping a dishrag across her eyes.

I lay on top of her while Paul pinched one quill at a time with the pliers and yanked. With each tug she went airborne and sent us both flying. We had to stop regularly to catch our breath and wipe up bloody saliva.

We fought that dog for hours, and got out a few quills. Sometime in the middle of the night, bruised and exhausted, we gave up and fell asleep on the floor.

In the morning, we medevaced her to Nome, a one-hundred-and-fifty-mile-round-trip taxi ride on a seasonal gravel road. The veterinarian who took over knocked her out and pulled more than one hundred and fifty quills, some of which were imbedded sideways and had to be cut out from the inside of her jowls.

As visions of the impending bill throbbed in my head, I started wondering: What was a porcupine doing out there on the tundra anyway? I always thought of them as woodland creatures.

In addition to fresh greens, porcupines nosh on the inner bark of trees not to mention boots, backpacks, ax handles, canoe paddles and outhouse seats. Urban porkys even nibble on car tires, lured by salt from the roads. But anyway, porcupines spend a fair amount of time up in trees—enough that they've earned a reputation for falling out of them.

Supposedly, porcupines have more going on upstairs than they lead us to believe.

Supposedly, they can escape from a cage faster than a monkey.

If porcupines are so smart, I wondered, what were they doing on the Seward Peninsula where there aren't any trees to fall out of?

Our field guides said they weren't supposed to be there. But porcupines aren't supposed to be in a lot of places where they've turned up.

In the Arctic. In desert regions. Even fourteen thousand feet up Mount Rainier once.

So having the little land mines out there on the windswept tundra apparently was no big stretch.

After giving Eva one last inspection, the vet lifted her to the floor. When she came to, eyes at half-mast, head hung groggily, she got to her feet, we headed out the door, and I loaded her into the back of the taxi for the long, bumpy ride home.

That evening, I took a moment to admire the porcupine's astounding capabilities—of being able to survive in such a harsh environment, of being able to mess up much bigger, badder animals without breaking a sweat.

And then I served Eva the last of the porcupine meat.

I assumed that would be the end of it, that she'd learned not to tangle with the things. But now this dog had one reason for living, and that was to even the score.

For the next ten years, she went after them with a vengeance. The more it hurt, the more determined she was to make the bastards pay. And she persuaded our other dog to become a wannabe assassin, too.

It's not that porcupines go looking for trouble. But when a wild animal's top speed is a waddle, it's only fair Nature would arrange for it to pack a piece.

Porcupines take life in the slow lane because they can. They're not exactly a favorite predator snack. With a few rare exceptions—a particularly adept or desperate bear, wolverine, or lynx—porcupines don't have much to fret about. Taking them on is almost always a losing proposition.

A biologist friend once found a wolf skull with quills imbedded in the roof of its mouth, evidence of a terrible death by starvation.

After leaving Teller, we returned to live in our off-the-grid cabin about a half-hour drive from downtown Fairbanks. That's where the porcupine wars began in earnest. We didn't let the dogs run loose, but now and then they'd get away and come back clobbered.

Once, a dog-sitter let them out of their pen; they bolted, and hours later came crawling home quilled. The anesthesia had barely worn off when, the very next day, they did it all over again. We returned from that trip to a $1,000 vet bill.

We could have put a kid through college with what we've spent on after-hours quill removal. Still, we could never shoot a porcupine the way one of our neighbors does: on sight. When porcupines wander into our yard, we just chase them (in slow motion) off the property, except the time Paul herded this big honker into a computer box and took it for a long ride before letting it go.

These porcupine wars of ours dragged on for years. The longer they did, the more I found myself rooting for the porcupine and less for the dumb dogs of the world and even less for the dumb dog owners who let those dumb dogs escape in the first place.

We're not the only boneheads. Longtime Anchorage veterinarian Jim Scott has pulled quills out of hundreds of dogs through the years. Sitting at his kitchen table one afternoon, he told me about a big old hound that managed to achieve payback nirvana by actually killing a porcupine. But even in death, the porcupine prevailed.

At the end of the battle, the hound's face looked like a porcupine with its quills on backward. It took Scott nearly five hours to pull them all. And the dog lost both his eyes.

Then Scott told me a much more pleasant story, one from the early 1970s, when people were bringing him injured and orphaned animals left and right: ravens, eagles, baby moose, black bear cubs.

One day this couple came into his clinic, pulled him aside, and asked in a whisper, "Ah, can we talk to you in private?"

They had with them a little box, and in it was a newborn porcupine. Its quills, soft at birth, had not even fully hardened yet.

They were embarrassed to say so, but they told him they liked porcupine meat. When a porcupine had wandered into their yard, the guy shot it in the head with a .22. Bending down beside it, he saw its belly wiggle, slit open the gut, and out popped this little bitty thing.

They both felt terrible and wondered if the good doctor would be willing to take care of the baby porky. He did.

Scott bottle-fed him and picked branches for him to chew on. He named him Pork, and when he called, Pork would come. Scott let him waddle around the clinic, and as long as he didn't back up, nobody got hurt.

After about two months, Pork had grown to the size of a small watermelon and was chewing on furniture and anything else he could sink his teeth into. When he started climbing, and stuff started crashing to the floor, it was time for him to go.

Scott hated to, but he carried him in his arms up into the Chugach Mountains, said goodbye, and set him free.

Now, every porcupine I see brings to mind Pork. It's all good, though, because finally, our household made peace with porcupines.

After too many years of this nonsense, a clay artist friend crafted a raku porcupine bust with wise eyes, magenta guard hairs, and gold-tipped shish kebab skewers as quills. We hung it in our living room as a talisman. And we haven't had bad porcupine juju since.

Calving

KARSTEN HEUER

Leanne bumped me for the umpteenth time as she shifted positions. "Are they still out there?" she asked.

I unfolded my knees and ankles as I carefully squeezed past the mound of gear she'd pushed aside in order to cook, then I leaned out the tent's door. Thirty yards away lay eight caribou cows waiting to give birth, while behind them stood two others, each nursing a wobblylegged calf.

"How many?" Leanne whispered after I'd nodded.

I squinted into the fog, trying to make out shadows and ghostlike shapes. Hundreds. Maybe thousands. For all I knew, every pregnant cow in the hundred-and-twenty-three-thousand-member herd was out there. Until the weather cleared, it was impossible to say.

We hadn't gone far after the pilot had dropped us off—five hundred yards, perhaps—before half a dozen cows had flushed out of the bushes and waddled off looking very pregnant and very agitated. Feeling terrible, we'd pitched camp right there despite the standing water, assuming the soggy campsite would suffice for a few hours until the animals drifted on. But then six cows became twelve, and the following hours brought dozens more. They'd lain down around us. They'd waited. And although more had arrived, none had moved off.

We had tried to go outside, but each attempt had set off a wave of panic among the cows. They were now, unlike in the spring migration, suddenly intolerant of our presence, skittish and paranoid, bolting from as far as a quarter mile away. It took a few tries before we realized what was happening. We couldn't continue walking—we couldn't even stretch. Those animals that had given birth were protective of their newborns, and those that hadn't were so vigilant and sensitive that we couldn't so much as stand upright and take a step. Surrounded by calving caribou, we had become hostages in our tent.

It was a position most wildlife photographers would die for, and yet we were miserable. After five days of sitting in Kaktovik, it was movement we craved, not more rest, a yearning that spun in our heads as much as itched in our feet. In less than a week, we'd been yanked from wilderness to industrial society and back again, and our spirits were struggling to adjust to the transitions that the plane and helicopter had rendered so abrupt. We were only fifty miles from where Walt had plucked us from the bank of the Kongakut River six days earlier, and yet everything had changed: the weather, the bird songs that filled the foggy air around us, the amount of snow, and the caribou themselves. Disoriented and unsettled, we wanted to walk again—to feel the rhythms that had helped connect us to the land and the caribou on their spring migration—but our ability to do so had changed as well.

"I'm going out to pee," said Leanne, starting out the back door. I nodded, holding a finger to my lips as she elbowed past, scrunching me against the wall. But she needed no reminding that caribou were right outside. Her knees hadn't even left the tent before she was crawling back inside.

"They're freaking out," she explained.

I gestured toward her cup as she crossed her legs in desperation. We'd both done it during the blizzard—saving the hassle of getting dressed to brave the elements—but those had been special circumstances. Now, Leanne refused—but after a half hour of waiting, she couldn't wait any longer.

"Let me get this straight," she said while hauling down her pants. "The oil companies figure they can build and operate airstrips here. They say they can have pumping stations, pipelines, roads, and drill pads and still not disturb the animals . . . but I can't even step outside this tent?"

I laughed, turning away to give her privacy, trying not to listen as our four-by-six-foot bedroom—which had now also become our living and eating area—became a bathroom as well.

It wasn't until the next morning that the fog and light rain lifted and, for the first time since stepping out of the helicopter four days before, we saw where we sat. An aqua blue river ran on one side of us, a low grassy bump rose up from the flat expanse of tussocks on the other, and straight ahead, stretching back into the straw-colored foothills of the Brooks Range, was a wide basin dotted with thousands of caribou. I looked up, way up, at the jagged white-and-blue peaks that towered as high as nine thousand feet behind them, and the value of this place hit home. Hemmed in by towering glaciers on one side and a frozen ocean on the other, the twenty-mile-wide coastal plain is a precious strip of fertile ground.

"Good morning," I beamed, kissing Leanne hard as she sat up and rubbed her eyes.

"Morning?" She looked at her watch. "It's 3:30 a.m."

"An exhilarating, wonderful, caribou-filled morning," I said, leaning toward her again. She deflected my second advance and leaned forward to peer out the door. Within seconds, she understood my sudden shift in mood.

Despite the hour, the sun was already climbing from its night run across the northern horizon, and all that had been drab and gray in the days before now glimmered in the early morning light. The brown grass had turned gold, the eyes of every caribou shone silver, and the buds on every bush hung like diamonds in the fiery, low-angle light. Even the sounds had changed: instead of the caws and screams of ravens and jaegers that had dominated the misty days before, the voices of songbirds now filled the air—Lapland longspurs, white-crowned sparrows, snow buntings, and horned larks—whistling and trilling to attract a mate.

"What's that?" whispered Leanne a few minutes later.

"What's what?" I asked. The place was layered in sound.

"That," said Leanne when something broke through the melodies. It wasn't a song she was referring to but a sputtering cough. Scanning every bush and hollow, we honed in on the hacking wheeze. Not forty yards away, a cow caribou lay on her side, panting on a patch of snow.

"She's in labor," whispered Leanne.

I nodded, hopeful that because the fog had lifted, we might actually see what transpired. A handful of other cows had reached the same point over previous days, but all had walked into the mist to give birth out of sight. Grabbing our respective cameras, we jostled for the best vantage, threw fingers for who got the tripod, then positioned ourselves at the door.

For the next half hour we watched as the cow rose, took a few steps, then dropped to the ground again, switching from one side to the other in an attempt to get comfortable. There were other cows in the vicinity, but they paid her little attention, continuing to graze and doze as they waited for their own time to come. Finally, after staggering from snow to wet tussocks and back again, the laboring cow found a rare patch of dry tussocks and settled in.

Compared to the hardships and effort the caribou had endured to get here, birth seemed remarkably quick and easy for her. Lying sideways, she looked once over her shoulder, gave a few pushes, then sent the dark, wet bundle into the world with one smooth heave.

"It's tiny," enthused Leanne as the cow rose and turned to lick the shiny, football-size calf clean. Behind the cow, the silvery rope of the broken umbilical cord swung against her bloodstained legs.

"And determined," I whispered as a miniature muzzle rose above the tussocks and suckled at the air in jerky sweeps. It disappeared for a moment, rose again, then climbed even higher as the calf struggled to its feet. Leanne looked up from the viewfinder in disbelief.

"It's already standing!"

Indeed, less than five minutes after being born, the calf had levered itself upright on what appeared to be a very generous helping of legs. It was comical how long they were—four stiltlike limbs wedged under a tiny body, each going its own way as new nerves short-circuited the fledgling muscles sheathed under a layer of short brown fur and paper-thin skin. Struggling for control, the calf pitched forward and toppled, staying on the ground only as long as it took to gather itself and try again.

It took three attempts to reach the fur of its mother's underbelly, two to find the udder, and one more to latch onto a teat, but when it did, there was no letting go. For the next few minutes Leanne and I watched as the calf's body gyrated with the flow of warm milk into its belly, quietly laughing as waves of pleasure ran the length of its quivering body, from slurping lips to the white, vibrating tail. I looked at my watch as the calf fed. Seventeen minutes had passed since it had been born. In another fifteen, it would take its first steps and a life of journeying would begin.

I don't know whether it was the beauty of the birth, the clearing weather, the remarkable views, or a mixture of all three that made the difference, but our spirits lifted that morning. For the first time in days, we didn't mind the sitting. In fact we relished it, for moving would have meant missing not only the calf's arrival but also the flush of life that came behind it. It was as if a switch had been thrown, releasing all the energy and potential that had gathered for weeks around us, sending it spilling onto the coastal plain. Killdeers, sandpipers, and other shorebirds flew in with brant geese on a wave of wings, while bees, butterflies, and swallows drifted and swooped in and out of view. It was a dance that everything was doing—the mergansers that glided in and plied the braided channels of the nearby river, the ground squirrels that darted in and out of their burrows, and the pair of longspurs that, after days of subdued courting, copulated in front of our tent in a sudden flutter of wings. Even the new caribou mothers had fresh energy, running ahead a few steps before stopping to encourage their newborns to follow, grunting and bobbing their approval with each of the calves' shaky steps.

Everything seemed to be celebrating life, to be rejoicing in its beauty, and we threw open the tent doors in an effort to be part of it all, marveling as clusters of Arctic poppies and mountain avens erupted in yellow and white blooms. We still couldn't move because of caribou, and we were still relegated to sitting, but it was no longer confining. Having been forced to watch, we couldn't help but appreciate what was happening around us. Because of the caribou, we'd stumbled onto the riches of being still.

There were hundreds if not thousands of calves outside our tent now, but it was the one whose birth we'd seen that Leanne and I watched closely, tracking its remarkable development for the next four days. By the end of one day it was walking, on the second day it started hopping, and by the third day it discovered how to translate those hops into forward propulsion, launching itself after real and imaginary playmates in what barely passed as a run. Such a spectacle of self-discovery was amusing for Leanne and me, but not for its mother. No sooner had she found the exploring calf and resumed her almost-constant grazing than the youngster was off again, necessitating a whole new round of grunts and head bobs to get it back. Gradually, after many such displays, a few scolds, and one or two charges from protective mothers that didn't appreciate its advances, the calf moderated its floppy-legged dashes and stuck closer to its mom. The all-important cow-calf bond was beginning to form.

A week of knocking elbows, rubbing shoulders, and poking one another with errant hands and clumsy feet had triggered another sort of bonding experience for Leanne and me inside the tent. Only, it wasn't what I'd expected. We hadn't bickered, there were no complaints, and aside from the occasional joke, neither of us protested too loudly about the other's increasingly strong smells. Instead, something special had developed: a kind of shared consciousness that, more than anything, could be attributed to constant touch.

No matter what the time of day, parts of us were always pressed together—arm to arm as we crouched in the doorway taking pictures, head to leg as one kept watch and the other read, back to belly as we spooned together in the sleeping bag. The restlessness that had typified the first days of being surrounded was gone, and the claustrophobia we'd felt while tent-bound in the spring migration during storms hadn't returned. We still tossed, turned, fidgeted, and readjusted, but it seemed smoother and more coordinated—as though our personal rhythms had fused into a subconscious dance. We awoke well rested, spent our waking hours knowing what the other was thinking, and, as the days progressed, found less and less need to talk. The effect was magical; inside the tent all went quiet, and outside, as the cows and calves discovered their own system of body language all around us, the barks, grunts, bleats, and huffs that had dominated the last few days gave way to a soft, milling hush.

Marooned

MICHAEL ENGELHARD

The students recline in a halfcircle in camp chairs facing the scalloped bay, afraid to miss out on the scenery. By week three of this thirty-day "ed-venture," companionship, paddling skills, and new landscapes have begun to fill any void TV or video games may have caused. Our surroundings help translate the course curriculum—Politics and Ecology of the Tongass National Forest—into realities that will become deeply ingrained, as memories. Luckily, no clearcuts dissect today's view. Hills dark with cedar, hemlock, and Sitka spruce wrap around the bases of sudden massifs. Peaks throng above the tree line and higher still, barbed vanes of cirrus. Along the shore's scrawl a dozen sea kayaks lie where we landed, beached like crayon-colored pilot whales. Gulls shriek in a winged blizzard near the high-water mark, pecking at dead things between the rocks. The tide carries notes of kelp, brine, mudflats, and decay—creation's inimitable perfume—while less than ten miles from us the hemisphere's southernmost tidal glacier dips its crystal tongue into the fjord. Mediterranean afternoons too rarely grace Alaska's Inside Passage; before we even pitch tents we take advantage of this one, teaching a lesson on glacial morphology. Lulled by the warmth and my co-instructor's voice, my concentration keeps slipping. A different form of attentiveness takes over as I scan the beach for bears on the prowl.

Some bright, medium-size animal *does* register in my field of vision, on an island afloat in the bay. Pacing from one end to the other, it appears to be testing the perimeter of its confinement. Could it be a wolf? I reach for my field glasses, tense enough to alert the group.

A head too small, and angular as slab marble, offsets a boulder-shaped body. Shag fluffs the creature's fore- and hindquarters into ridiculous bloomers. A mountain goat. At sea level. The incoming tide has barred its retreat, stranding it like an ice chest washed off some tour boat or a bergy bit gone astray. At first glance it could be a billy or nanny. Both sexes sport jet black spikes, which local Tlingit Indians carve into potlatch spoons—curved, functional, keratin art. According to our guidebooks, adult male goats are the ones most likely to go gallivanting, from alpine reaches down crenellated ridges and into the shelter of conifers, lured by any ungulate tough's Promised Land: salt licks, or deep meadows to browse and populate. Elusive as well as exclusive, the white ghost of the Coast Range was not described scientifically until 1900 and claims a genus all to itself. Earlier encounters with body parts had resulted in misunderstandings; on his journey along this rugged littoral, Captain Cook traded for mountain goat hides, attributing them to "glacier" bears.[6]

The students are standing now, firn lines and medial moraines temporarily consigned to their minds' garrets. Our intern, Neil, sprints to his kayak, slides into the cockpit, and, pushing with the palms of his hands, seal-launches from the beach.

"What are you going to do?" someone shouts. "Drape it across your bow?"

"Don't know," he replies. "Just taking a closer look, I guess."

Why not leave it be? I wonder. What feeds this need for proximity, this urge to interfere? We nurse oil-slicked otters and eagles back to health. We radio-collar caribou to understand timeless but timed wanderings. We keep bears in cages, to edify, engage, enchant, entertain. We make room for wolves where we used to poison them and, just as absurdly, installed mountain goats in Nevada and Colorado, where trophy hunters can chase them. Regardless of its motivation, the reaching-out of a species that exiled itself behind barriers of artifice can be a bleak and beautiful thing. I only hope nobody will suffer injury or indignity on this occasion.

While Neil disembarks on the low-slung island, the goat gallops up and over a rise. Neil walks to the top, neoprene skirted, paddle in hand, to see what we have already seen from shore: the goat churning toward an outcrop nearby, muzzle pointed skyward, cutting a wake like a chunky retriever.

By the time Neil has inserted himself in the kayak again, the billy has climbed its miniature Ararat, which soon will submerge. Against the sea's backdrop, the animal seems out of its element but still more of this place than we Goretex-clad visitors from afar. Possessed of a mineral quality, a poise and resilience older than flesh, it stands riveted to rock—an extension of sweeping summits, hewn from Le Conte Glacier's trunk, hefty and blunt as winter itself. Its stubborn form embodies the land's pluck and fiber. Like snowfields crisp in the distance or the void on explorers' charts, the goat not only invites speculation but even more so the projection of desires. I would trade with this bearded recluse in an instant. I'd travel unburdened by gear. I'd grow hairy and hunchbacked and rank. I'd become agile enough to dodge grizzlies and wolves, fearless enough to bed down on vertiginous ledges—and smart enough to avoid our kind.

With a lapse into pastoral metaphor excusable in a Scotsman, wilderness sage John Muir compared this breed to others of "nature's cattle," considering none better fed or protected from the cold. But he also acknowledged the grit in their existence. During a sledding trip above Glacier Bay, on the ice flow that still bears his name, he found bones cast about in an ancient blood ritual. Their configuration spelled out the death of a frail or sick or unlucky one. Presumably, wolves had caught up with a wild goat two miles from safer ground, where breakneck terrain matched with ballerina grace would have given it the advantage. Despite their famed surefootedness, missteps occur, and the abyss claims its share of mountain goats every year. Loose rocks and avalanches strike down others. Inexperienced kid goats may fall to the talons of golden eagles, which hunt alone or pair up to corner them.

Current logging practices in the Tongass—stripping its slopes of cover and feed—further skew the odds against survival in the margins.

Pulling away from these sobering thoughts, I watch Neil bump the outcrop with the bow of his kayak. He waves a paddle blade in the animal's face. What is he doing? Trying to save a goat by making it dive? It's unlikely to drown, even if it gets flooded out. But Neil might yet discover the flip side of hands-on approaches to learning. If the goat chooses to answer intrusion with uncivil disobedience, our rookie instructor will have a hard time explaining hoof marks on his kayak deck back at the warehouse.

Clearly annoyed with being crowded, the billy indeed takes him on, defending its quickly shrinking domain. It jerks horn daggers into Neil's direction, hooking the air, unwilling to yield as much as an inch.

On shore, the students holler and cheer—for whom, I cannot tell.

Eventually, the goat's aversion to humans overcomes any fear of tiderips, reefs, or the unfamiliar. Shoulders tucked in like a boxer, it pivots and leaps high and wide, charging its twin in the burnished sea. Before long we lose sight of it as it dog-paddles across the bay, to be culled from the gene pool or to sire a feisty clan somewhere in the high country.

The Woman Who Gardens with Bears

ANA MARIA SPAGNA

At certain times of the year, my partner, Laurie, faces a unique job
hazard when the orchard she maintains becomes, as she puts it, a
Slip 'n Slide. The local black bears that gorge themselves on apples for
several hours a day leave enough scat in sloppy mounds that you can't take
three steps without landing in it. It's slippery when it's fresh in August, and
it's slipperier in March when the snow melts and the preserved mounds,
hundreds of them over three acres, reappear sporting a furry mold. So
Laurie not only has to watch her step, she has to watch her balance. If it's
an unusual hazard, hers is an unusual job.

The historic orchard—three hundred aging apple trees preserved for
posterity by the feds—is set in the oxbow of a wild mountain river running
fast and glacial blue at the base of granite cliffs rising steep. The scenery is
stunning, the ancient trees hearty, the apples organically grown and free to
any picker. From the moment Laurie began, she loved her job: the gnarly,
scabby-barked trees, the shovel-alone independence, even the challenges—
which came in spades.

For starters, the ditches. Miles of open ditches—*rills*, they're called—
drew snowmelt down from the peaks, over a waterfall, under a small road
bridge, and eventually between the rows of trees, soaking the roots at the
drip line. Or at least, that was the idea. The ditches were clogged with silt
and gravel, with cottonwood shoots, blackberry vines, and Oregon grape

roots that sank and spread thick as cruise ship moorings. Laurie shoveled the gravel and chopped the roots, then ran a weedeater until her hands vibrated to numbness and water ran free.

That is, the water ran free but it couldn't reach the tree roots. Orchard grass carpeted the sandy loam like a too-effective trade embargo. Laurie tried breaking the sod with a shovel. No go. Chopping with a Pulaski worked better but was too slow. Finally, she used a backhoe bucket to peel back the sod and make way for the water and, in no time flat, for an onslaught of aggressive weeds—knapweed, rush skeletonweed, toadflax, salsify—which, in turn, she had to battle. Since the orchard was organic, herbicides were out and ditto for pesticides.

And there were pests aplenty: ants, aphids, caterpillars, woodpeckers. Bigger pests, too: deer standing on their hind legs to eat low-hanging leaves, elk gnawing on bark, girdling the trunks, and midsummer tourists crawling all over the place.

The job was an intricate balancing act, and, when on balance, the act worked. Laurie sprayed soapy water on aphids, and she burned tent caterpillars with a propane torch. She tossed the one-year-old whips from her summer pruning to the deer. She sicced a neighbor dog on the mice—six in one day—and watched a raven chase the dog away. Everything in the orchard lived in tenuous harmony. With one exception.

The bears, save the poop, were hard to see. A branch swayed on a windless day. A green apple thunked to the ground. Finally you'd spot them wobbling on the twiggiest limbs reaching for apples, taking one bite and tossing them down, knocking more to the ground in the process. They're wasteful, one neighbor always said, as if that were the worst part of the quandary, that the bears didn't clean their plates. Then the branch would splinter or peel away and dangle grotesquely. The bear would stumble off like a drunkard, and the tree likely would never recover.

Make no mistake, the bears needed no sympathy. They didn't need the orchard to survive anymore than humans did. There was plenty for them to eat in the hills: huckleberries, saskatoons, mountain ash. Lots and lots of ants. But the bears preferred the orchard. Apples, after all, are a lot bigger than ants. The bears liked it there, and Laurie liked it, too, so that first season, she put up with them.

During the second season, their numbers increased. Some people said six. Some counted eight. Some claimed as many as thirteen black bears frequented the orchard. An especially large male slept, day after day, in a ponderosa next to where Laurie parked her bicycle, his body draped over a beefy limb eighty feet up. Visitors stepped off the tour bus and walked right under him.

"Have you seen any bears?" they asked.

Laurie never let on that one lounged right overhead. She looked forward to the day when scat would splat and the secret would be out.

"Nope," she said.

One hot day in August, I brought Laurie lunch. She'd been running the backhoe, and she shut it off to sit with me for a while in the shade. Shortly after we sat, we spotted a sow and a cub wandering, wet and dreamy, like a couple of love-struck characters in a TV mini drama. They had swum the river and were following their noses, as bears are always following their noses, but they looked lost, purposeless, as they stumbled from the frothy river through a dry pasture and into Shangri La, an apple orchard, three hundred trees nearly ripe. The sow looked as though she'd found the mother lode—Eureka!—and wasted no time clambering into a tree and shaking armloads of apples to the ground. *Kathump, kathump, kathump.*

I laughed.

Laurie scowled.

We looked around for the cub, but he seemed to have disappeared, so Laurie gulped the last of her coffee.

"I've got to get back to work," she said.

We walked together through tall grass and a swarm of black flies that glommed onto Laurie, spinning circles around her head, and we headed toward the big ponderosa where I'd parked my bike next to hers. As we passed the backhoe, we saw the cub at last, curled into a ball in the bucket, warming itself in the sun.

"You have to admit he's awfully cute," I said.

Laurie just shook her head.

I looked up at the big male sleeping on the overhead limb and pedaled away.

The problem was getting out of hand. Bears dominated conversations throughout the valley. One afternoon our friend Chad, a Texan and a West Point grad, came upon a sow lazing on his front porch beside a shredded screen door. Inside two cubs stood on their tiptoes on the white Formica counter and reached up to topple bags of pancake mix and dried hummus out of the cabinets. Chad was neither scared nor amused. He left the sow oblivious on the porch and raced in the back door with a clublike maple limb to chase the mewing cubs back through the shaggy screen into the hot sun.

His housemate was appalled.

"Don't you want your grandkids to see a bear?" she asked.

"Not in their kitchen," Chad answered.

Historically, of course, bears in the orchard were shot, more than sixty in one season, according to local myth. Even now shooting them was not entirely out of the question. Hunting was legal almost everywhere in the valley. Except for the orchard. Maybe that was because of the close proximity to homes. More likely it was because it would not be fair to get the bears addicted to apples, then kill them.

But that's what happened anyway. The bears got used to humans in the orchard, then they moved on to nearby houses where they ravaged gardens and sniffed out garbage and sneaked through cat doors. When eventually they got too greedy, when their preference for human food made them too daring and foolhardy, they were shot by homeowners who didn't need a permit to defend person or property. And it all started in the orchard. Solutions abounded—a fence for one thing—but none of the bureaucrats could stomach the suggestion.

"Have you seen any bears?" a new ranger asked Laurie, feigning interest in helping her herd them away.

Laurie began to explain her plan to fence them out, and he interrupted. "But my kids sure love seeing them."

She couldn't win.

Chad, for his part, didn't worry much about to-fence or not-to-fence. He'd learned to use a rifle back at West Point, and he was at wit's end. With a little prodding from Laurie and me, he bought a bear tag and borrowed our pickup. It did not take long before the big male that slept in the ponderosa ventured out in search of water or newly arrived salmon and passed outside the orchard boundary where Chad lay in wait. When Chad returned the pickup to us, he was elated. The bear, he figured, had weighed over three hundred pounds. He planned to have a rug made for his dad back in San Antonio.

"Do you want to come over for dinner next week and try the backstrap? Best meat you'll ever taste."

"Sure," I said. "Sure."

But Laurie wasn't looking at him. She was staring at the two-by-eight tailgate board now stained with blood, and she kept staring in silence as Chad pedaled away on his bike to go finish the butchering. I knew what was up: blood on our tailgate meant blood on our hands, and as much as she wanted those bears dead, she couldn't shake the unease.

Still, Laurie wasn't ready to give up. The bears continued to wreak havoc in the orchard, swinging from branches, sauntering across the rills, posing, it seemed, for photographs each time the tour bus pulled in. Visitors flocked in from miles away, ecstatic at the sight.

"Are you The Woman Who Gardens with Bears?" one asked, meaning well, making a joke.

Laurie was not amused. She considered putting up a sign that read WELCOME TO THE PETTING ZOO.

Instead, she decided to help our chicken-keeping neighbors butcher the birds, thinking that maybe after practicing on chickens, she might be able to get a tag and kill a bear herself. But it didn't work. She didn't mind the blood and guts, but she couldn't stand the palpable terror when the chickens raced about the pen trying not to get caught. She wondered what they were thinking.

"They don't have very big brains," the chicken-keeping neighbor assured her.

That didn't make her feel much better, at least not about the bears that seemed to have slightly bigger brains than chickens. After all, Laurie spent a lot of time with the bears. Her relationship with them was complicated. Sure, she'd feel bad killing them, but she felt worse about luring them in— baiting them, feeding them, spoiling them, making them less what they ought to be—and worse yet about the simple truth: she loved the apple trees more than the bears. For nearly everyone else it was the other way around: they loved the bears more than the trees.

She'd never win, she figured. She might as well give up.

Twelve years later, though the job is seasonal and offers no security, Laurie is still at it. Each year several more trees die; most years a bear or two gets killed. The bears move slowly, though not methodically. They are haphazard, distracted by whatever comes their way, and for all their ferocious image, most often they seem surprised by humans—even by Laurie, day after day. They give her that look: what are *you* doing here? They can climb with alacrity, and sometimes run fast, but usually they don't. They choose not to. They hang out, going nowhere. They're not natural in the orchard, and someday they might get fenced out, but for now, that's where they'll stay.

Meanwhile, Laurie slips and slides through the scat. Applesauce, she calls it. She watches bears climb, and she tries to keep tourists a safe distance away. She yells at the bears and throws rocks. She tried a slingshot, but now uses a high-powered shotgun with rubber bullets, beanbags, and firecrackers. The strategy works for keeping the bears out in the daytime, which limits the damage they do the trees to half and disappoints a lot of gawkers and maybe saves a bear or two's life. But it doesn't save the apples. The better cultivated the crop, the more apples there are, so the more apples the bears eat. The last few years there have been none—zip, zero, *nada*—left for humans.

"How is the apple crop looking, Laurie?" people like to ask. It is the question Laurie hears most often, she says, and the one she hates second most.

"The bears got them," she says.

Their eyes light up, and they forget what they were asking about.

"Have you seen any bears?" they ask.

That's the question Laurie hates most.

Each year in August when the bears arrive, Laurie hardly sleeps. And I don't know what to do to help. Last year, I bought an inflatable kayak, hoping that floating the river on the weekends might distract her. And it did, a little, until one day in September.

We were driving home from the orchard watching autumn sunlight slip behind yellow larches on the ridgetops and the river water ripple—running too low this year, too low as always—when suddenly, near our driveway, a wiggly rumped bear appeared, coming toward us on the dusty road.

"What's up with him, you think? Shouldn't he be down at the orchard gorging himself?"

"Probably just curious, checking out the neighborhood. He's pretty cute, don't you think?"

"What?" I was aghast. I could not believe that, after all those years of fretting and complaining, she could say such a thing.

"You have to admit that little guy is cute," she said.

We'd spooked him with our pickup and he scampered down the valley behind us. In the rearview mirror I watched his haunches rolling like shoulders shrugging in a heavy coat.

"I guess," I said.

We pulled into the driveway beside the place where our new blue boat sat amongst the Shasta daisies, ready and waiting for the weekend—but looking a little lopsided, one whole side deflated, entirely flat. I hopped out to take a closer look and found tooth marks galore, still wet with slobber. The little bear had been curious all right: there were twenty-six holes in all.

"Still think he's cute?" I asked.

"Yeah," Laurie said. "I do."

In a few short weeks, the orchard would collect cold air sinking, the first place in the valley to freeze hard. The few remaining apples would be nabbed, and the insatiable bears would wade out onto sandbars to gorge on spawned-out salmon, while Laurie worked alone, preparing the trees for winter, cold fingers fumbling, waiting to be laid off. Then the bears would sleep hard in their secret dens, having waited for the late-arriving snow to cover their tracks, while Laurie sat at the kitchen table peeling apple bark with a grafting knife from sawed-off limbs to use as door handles or coat hooks. Eventually, before spring, it would fall on her to patch the twenty-six holes in the heavy rubber kayak. I wouldn't have the patience. I don't know anyone else who would.

FEATHERS

Raven

CAROLYN SERVID

On the slope of a hill in the center of town, a lone, tall cottonwood's bare boughs straggle out into a dark November dawn. A congregation has been gathering at the old tree, twenty-four, five, six black silhouettes against the slowly fading edge of night. They come silently and sit silently, each finding a place, near one another but not too close. There is a deep red promise of daylight in the east.

Another glides in, settles in the sprawling branches. In a few minutes, another does, easing himself down through the air onto a small high limb. No one says a word. Though the town is starting to come to life in the dusky morning—a few cars and pickups idling at the traffic signal, a cyclist pedaling through the green light, a beeping garbage truck backing up, a man walking his dog—the silence in the venerable tree holds its own space in the chill air.

I stand across the street below, looking up thirty feet into the cottonwood, watching the conclave. Ravens, *Corvus corax*, the region's quintessential bird. Raven the intelligent one, the opportunist, the schemer. Raven the vocalist, the scavenger, the aeronautic acrobat. Raven the playful bird, the loyal mate, the everyday black form perched or flying or walking or calling. Raven the creator, the trickster, the regal one atop totems, on sacred robes and helmets and hats. Ravens, thirty now, still silent, gathered in the half-light of early morning.

They congregate here most every day in the awakening interlude between darkness and daylight, an intentional meeting it seems, not an accidental one. It's as though they're checking in with each other after being separated for several hours of darkness, a roll call of sorts. Where have they each spent the night? Do they recognize each other? How much do they know about each other? Do the same birds come every day? I wonder. Perhaps they're scoping out plans for the day. Perhaps elders are there to take younger ones under wing; perhaps rivals are there to check out competitors. Or perhaps they've gathered to share information.

On some impulse one takes flight, dropping down on spread wings, gliding over my head, tail spread, black pinion feathers tipped up, swooping past me into the alley of space above the street between the tall apartments and St. Michael's Cathedral. I watch him disappear, imagine his flight down the street as an early reconnaissance of downtown. In a few minutes, a dark form flies back from that direction and settles in the tree. The others are still there. The eastern sky is rosy now and brightness is inching this way.

As the sky lightens, one raven starts talking. Not loud, not musically, just a simple *kraak* repeated every five or ten seconds. No one responds, but a few other birds start venturing out, one more heading downtown, another toward the harbor, another back toward the trees behind town. A couple of them seem to circle and return. The talker flies off, vocalizing as he goes. More follow his lead, others sit still, quiet, but the gathering is clearly breaking up. Soon only a dozen birds remain, and by the time daylight has filled the sky, they are all off on their ravenly ventures. I hear them now, in the distance, calling here, calling there. *Kraak! Kraak!*

According to Tlingit mythology it was Raven who brought daylight to a dark world. It took trickery and a child's temper, but neither was beyond him. In one version of the story recorded in Sitka he turned himself into a floating speck of dirt and impregnated a young woman who drank the raven-tainted water. The girl's father was a noted man from far up the Nass River whose hoarded treasures included the box of daylight. His daughter gave birth to a bright-eyed baby, born on a bed of moss. This grandson became a demanding young child who cried and cried until he was given what he wanted—first a bundle containing the stars, then another that held the moon, both of which he released through a smoke hole into the sky. His final fit of wailing got him what he wanted most—daylight tied up in a special box that he took with him as he flew out the smoke hole.

As the Sitka story goes, Raven ventured on and came to a town whose people had never seen daylight. He approached through the darkness and asked for help getting across a creek into town. When the people refused, he threatened them with daylight. Not knowing who he was or where he came from, they doubted and questioned him. To prove himself, Raven tweaked open the box just a crack, letting loose a flood of light so bright it practically threw the people to the ground. He quickly shut the box, but the townspeople only became more quarrelsome. Piqued with anger, Raven threw the lid wide open, releasing the sun into the sky. Full daylight was too much. It forced those townspeople who had skins of sea animals into the ocean and those with skins of land animals into the forest. They became the creatures whose skins they wore.

The contemporary English word *raven* comes from Old English *hraefn*, which is akin to Old High German *hraban* and Old Norse *hrafn*. Say any of them out loud, moving the *r* to the back of your throat, and you find yourself sounding a bit like a raven. Listen to Tlingit language being spoken and it's not hard to understand the legend I once heard that Raven taught the Tlingit to speak. Their language includes hard consonants that come from the back of the throat, others that are softened by the tongue, slight puffs of air, and varied use of high and low tones to impart different meanings. It is one of the most complex and difficult languages in the world.

Ravens have a greater range of vocalizations than any other bird. They croak and cluck and caw and gurgle and yell. They *prrruk* and squawk and squeal and mew. And they imitate other sounds. One summer evening, in the woods behind our house, a hermit thrush rippled the soft, fading light with his glass-flute melody, the first pure note as clear as still water, the following cascade floating down as easily as ripples moving along a stream. In a nearby tree, a raven listened, then tried his own version of hermit thrush song, a wobbly lyric that fluttered in the evening air with effort and no grace. The thrush sang on, his lilting melody repeating at one pitch, then another. Raven tried again, his throat too big for the thrush's subtle sounds, but still he floated his version, wavering erratic notes somewhere between a warble and a croak. Hermit thrush sang on, as though oblivious to raven, focused on his own domain. Raven hesitated, then tried again, the thrush's elegant clarity still out of reach. The counterpoint went on, thrush, raven, thrush, raven, thrush, thrush, raven, raven, thrush, thrush, thrush—*Kraak!* The mimicking raven gave up and flapped away into the forest.

My father visited me my first year in Alaska when I lived in a primitive cabin. During his visit we had to fix the gravity-fed water pipe that came from a small creek on the hillside, and we traipsed through the woods, looking for a breach in the line. In the near distance, a raven gurgled. "I hear water, my father said." I'd been fooled before myself, but not this time. "It's raven," I said and explained. He listened again and smiled in wonder. As we traipsed on, I outlined for him the Tlingit story—how creator Raven stole water from Petrel and distributed it in the rivers and streams, how Raven got stuck trying to fly out of Petrel's smoke hole, how Petrel stoked his fire with smoky wood, turning the once-white raven into the sooty black bird he is today.

Eyewitness: On a sloped roof, covered in fresh white snow, jet black raven just below the roofline, walking a few steps, head cocked down the angled pitch of new snow. He then lay down on his side, wings tucked, body parallel to the slope, and began to roll, slowly at first, then picking up a bit of speed—three rolls, four, five six seven to the lower edge of the roof where he stopped, got his feet under him, and strutted back up the slope to roll down again. Another winter, a different snow-covered roof, another raven engaged in the same black-on-white, snow-rolling play.

And on snow-covered ground beneath some trees, the white-feathered arc left by raven's black wing, a sweeping geometry that moved the bird into flight.

On a distant beach, in Haida mythic time, creator Raven in his wanderings came across a giant clamshell. Curious about faint sounds coming from within it, he looked more closely and found it full of tiny two-legged creatures, the first humans. Frightened by Raven and the vastness of the world, the little humans cowered inside their shell until, as Haida artist Bill Reid put it, "The Raven leaned his great head close to the shell and with the smooth trickster's tongue . . . he coaxed and cajoled and coerced the little creatures to come out and play in his wonderful, shiny, new world."[7]

A different beach in contemporary human time. Starrigavan Estuary north of Sitka, early morning, spring. I'd come in search of migrating shorebirds—yellowlegs, curlews, dunlins, godwits, the rare red knot—but there were only a few elusive sandpipers at the wave-lapped edge of the reaching tide flat. I ambled over rocks and wet sand, eyes down, watching my step, as I headed back toward the forested high tide line. When I looked up I saw my companion. Raven, poking around on a stretch of mudflat, wandering from spot to spot, head cocked this way and that, until something caught his interest. He stopped, pushed his beak down into the sand, and began to pull, first in short tugs, then a slower, steadier effort, bracing himself with his feet for leverage. Pull, *pull*, then a sharp tug and he had it, a crab, three to four inches across its back, its legs flailing, all except the one that raven held in his beak. He made quick work of his catch—got the body under his feet, yanked off one leg after another, tossing them carelessly aside, then dug his beak into the soft underbelly for a fresh feast.

What signal, what hint in the sand, told raven the crab was there? I wondered as he abandoned the carapace and wandered watchfully, curiously, about. Soon he stopped, renewed his concentration on a different spot, then pushed his beak into the sand again, deeper, and started to pull. No short tugs this time. Up against more resistance, he strained with his whole body, neck stretched out, feet pushing against the sand, shoulders and chest pulling, pulling, pulling, pulling—hah! A larger crab, more than four inches across, not willing to give itself up, its pinchers clawing the air, at raven, who ignored them, secured the crab's body with his feet, and quickly dispatched each leg, small ones first, then the larger, clawed feet. A litter of crab legs around him, he clasped the body in his sturdy beak, lifted off, and flew into the forest with his prize.

The word *raven* is also a verb: to take away by force, to devour hungrily or greedily.

Eyewitness: Two ravens side by side on the ridgeline of a roof, black feathers filling out their bodies, shoulders almost touching. One turns to the other and begins. Carefully, gently, that strong beak probes the partner's feathers, along one shoulder, up the neck a bit, across the upper back. The subject sits still, accepting, lowers its head and lets the grooming raven move down its back, then opens a wing, slightly, to the gently probing beak. No talk between them. Just this caretaking, this preening, one of the other. A private moment there, in the open, a quiet intimacy between these two birds, black eyes glistening, black feathers layered thickly over their taut bodies, black beaks silent to my ears, though who knows what muted sounds of satisfaction might have passed between them. Are they mates, these two, having chosen each other for life as ravens are said to do? Or is this some other relationship?

And just now, as the morning sky brightens, a raven calls from the trees of the cemetery at the end of our street, a grove that shelters the nest of a mated pair. *Krak tadak. Krak tadak. Krak tadak,* a three-syllable, rhythmic call, as though it were a particular signal or word. Who is listening? Who hears the call and responds?

Sitka National Historic Park harbors a spruce-and-hemlock forest that skirts a stretch of saltwater shoreline and shelters Indian River, once known as Kaasda Heen, where it flows into a tidal estuary and joins the waters of Sitka Sound. The park occupies land that traditionally belonged to the Kiks.ádi, one of the Raven clans of Sitka's Tlingit people. It commemorates the historic site of Shis'kí Noow, the Kiks.ádi fort at the mouth of Kaasda Heen, and the battleground on a nearby tidewater beach where the Kiks.ádi staged their last armed resistance in 1804 against Russian moves to colonize their homeland.

The park hosts a collection of totem poles, most of them brought to Sitka in the early 1900s from Tlingit and Haida villages south of Sitka, but there are a few newly carved ones as well. In the clearing where Shis'kí Noow once stood, the K'alyáan pole carved in 1999 now stands in memory of the Kiks.ádi who lost their lives in the 1804 battle. It is named after K'alyáan, the legendary Kiks.ádi warrior who, wearing a Raven helmet, led the charge against the Russians. The helmet is replicated at the bottom of the pole, held carefully by Frog, the clan crest of the Kiks.ádi. Above Frog and K'alyáan's helmet rise other Raven clan figures—Beaver, Dog Salmon, Sockeye Salmon, Woodworm. Atop them all sits Raven himself, invoked by his people, honoring his people.

And along the trail that circles the park there is Raven alone, steadfast, atop a memorial pole carved to pay tribute to another who had passed on—Raven with wings held back just a bit, his full breast bared, his heart open.

One afternoon, a clan of forty or more ravens had gathered at the park. I began to hear them as I walked along the trail, individual birds perched here, there, calling back and forth with clear, dark voices. Then I tuned in to the cacophony overhead in higher branches and above the trees. Raucous *caws*, desperate *kraas*, agitated *kraaks*. The ruckus was intense, like a crowd had gathered at a protest, was witnessing some unsettling event, or was wrestling with itself over some heated issue. In the air overhead, the flurried beating wings of ravens in flight, squawking as they flew. *Krak! Krak! Krak! Krak! Krak! Krak!* Their loud, throaty voices rose above and against each other. I could see their dark forms moving through the air above the trees, ten, twenty birds in flight. I moved out to the open beach for a better view: more ravens than I had imagined, flying in pairs, chasing each other in looping ellipses over the park's forest, from one end to the other, occasionally veering out over the beach only to cut back into the trees. Back and forth, round and round, frantically flying and shouting at each other, scolding each other, arguing with each other, teasing each other. Other ravens offered their own loud comments from perches, their voices a steady backdrop for the agitation of the birds in flight. Black-feathered forms, black wings, sharp black beaks, glassy black eyes, black feet, black voices, all in motion, all loudly alive. What? What? What?! I wanted to holler back at them. What *is* it?

Another afternoon, a lone raven on the park beach, walking along barnacled stones, unfazed by the uneven terrain, circling and zigzagging over a small stretch, alert to possibilities in the rocks. He walks silently, now and then probing with his beak between stones into tidal water where morsels of one sort or another may be hidden. Another raven calls from the forest edge. Beach raven looks up, answers briefly, then continues walking. His feet easily grab the contours of the stones. Downy tibial feathers on his legs make him look like he's wearing knee-length pants. His long tail waddles side to side with each step. Confident, this lone bird. He turns and the light catches his scallop-feathered nape and mantle, an elegant pattern of small feathers intricately layered on top of each other, a royal black cloak around his shoulders. From under this cloak, the long, tapered feathers of his wings glide down his back and sides, tucked tidily in just now. His tail feathers barely clear the beach. Head cocked inquisitively he stops, pokes his beak between stones, digs a bit deeper, pushes one stone aside with a deft flick of his head, looks up and shakes salty water off his beak, digs again, pulls up a treasure and holds it tentatively in his beak. I strain to see what it is, can only make out a bit of white I assume is a shell, and now expect him to fly up and drop it on the rocks to crack it open. Instead, he discards it, digs again, and pulls up another that he swallows whole, then picks up the first again and swallows it too. My eyes stretch wide in wonder. What did I see? He doesn't wait for me to figure it out. In one motion, he opens his wings, pushes off with his legs, and takes to the air. I hear him pump his wings—*fwhooo fwhooo fwhooo*—and watch his primary feathers stroke the air, his wedge tail flick and angle, his silhouette bank away over the trees.

At dusk, as darkness settles into the forest, two ravens, agitated, cackle at each other as though settling a difference, getting things straight between them before the night quiets them, before their forms disappear into dark trees, dark clouds, dark sky. Black on black, coal-bright eyes watching, then closing into sleep, waiting for morning's first hint of daylight.

The Voice of Home

HANK LENTFER

Twice a year, sandhill cranes flood the sky above my home. They drift in waves of loose flocks, tired after a long day's flight, wings set against a sunset sky. Just before touching down they flap heavily to slow the pull of gravity, gangly legs outstretched to meet the earth. On the ground they give up grace, collapse their elegant wings, and walk with an awkward, stilted step. In a few twilight hours the quiet wetlands west of our house are blanketed with chattering gray bodies. If the winds are still, I can hear their distant voices through the night. From my porch, the gathered birds sound like the burbling of a hundred gentle streams.

They might stay for a day, sometimes a week, waiting for fair winds and bright sun to build rising thermals. Their chatter increases through the morning until one bird crouches and leaps to the air, followed by another and another and a thousand more. They flap and glide in a growing spiral, falling slowly through the fast-rising air, calling incessantly as if lifted by their own sound. Lying on my back, attention drawn like gravity in reverse, I stare into the bowl of sky alive with a whirlpool of shape and sound.

At the thermal's top, the cranes spill out in long, fluid skeins, flowing with the current of a collective compass. In formation, the raucous cries quiet to the occasional call passed up and down the line. Not until the last bird slips from view and the last voice pulls beyond the straining reach of my ears do I get up, brush the grass from my shirt, and try to remember what I was doing with my day.

For decades I have lived beneath this spectacle. I hope to die here, too. The passage of seasons is shared with my wife, Anya, and now Linnea Rain, our four-year-old daughter. We live at the forested edge of a wide meadow along a stream that flows into a strait leading to the Gulf of Alaska. With a winter population of three hundred, some people call Gustavus a small town. Our mayor wants it to grow. I'm content with what we have; there's no need to get caught up in the biggering-and-bettering frenzy sprawling across the rest of the country.

We are not looking for fast food or fine arts. We're happy to carry our water in buckets, our firewood in our arms, and get an early morning feel for the weather on the way to the outhouse. We built our little sixteen-by-sixteen-foot cabin ourselves, pounding the rough boards together with nails and the naïve belief that, by staying put, we could somehow escape the urbanization of America. When my love affair with cranes started, I had no idea they would lead me to the very thing I was trying to avoid.

Ten million years ago, a roiling cloud of ash obliterated the sun and poured from the sky like an avalanche of black snow. It fell fast, trapping animals of the Great Plains where they stood, buried from the bottom up in ten feet of abrasive powder. Today, patient paleontologists pick apart the story of those creatures entombed in pulverized rock.

At an excavation site in Nebraska, teams of graduate students slowly scrap and sweep through the black earth surrounding an ancient watering hole. The world that emerges beneath their tools looks more like the African savanna than the farm country of the Midwest. They have unearthed an entire herd of hippos gathered for a drink. Around the outskirts of the oasis are the remains of rhinos, three-toed horses, deer-like animals with twisting, forward-leaning horns, and long-necked camels larger than present-day giraffes. The fine ash yields the delicate details of bones and even the impression of feathers from birds smothered alongside the mammals. Of all the bizarre critters rising from that ash, only the graceful skeleton of the sandhill crane looks familiar to our modern-day eyes.

Since that blast, cranes have made millions of migrations over a changing continent. Most of the species that survived the volcano were later killed by a prolonged drought that shuffled the composition of North American fauna. The cranes watched the demise of rhinos, camels, and hippos. They watched trans-American forests and woodlands give way to grassland prairie. They saw glaciers stretch from coast to coast, retreat and return, again and again. They witnessed the arrival and extinction of woolly mammoths and short-faced bears, saber-toothed tigers and giant sloths. Crane calls greeted the hunters and gatherers spreading south down the continent from Beringia. In recent decades, they watched the lights of cities scatter across the country like embers from a great fire. Whether cranes, the oldest birds on the planet, can survive this latest transformation of the continent is a question I hope remains unanswered in my lifetime.

Last fall, on a rare sunny day, I rode my bike to the Beartrack Mercantile, the town's one general store. Puddles from the morning rain steamed in the afternoon heat. Yellow cottonwood leaves, tugged by a growing breeze, drifted down in twisting flight. At the store, I bought a lime popsicle and joined several neighbors and a few late-season tourists lounging on the porch swing, leaning against dusty trucks, and sitting on the steps. Buoyed by the sun, the banter was quick and light. We heard the cranes moments before they poured into view. Hundreds of birds, winging just above the treetops, sprayed the parking lot with shadow and song. Not until they passed, pulling their blanket of sound with them, did I realize everyone was silent.

"Goddamn, that was something," said a fisherman in camo pants, uncomfortable with the sudden quiet. "What the hell were they?"

"Those are the reasons we live here," answered my neighbor Kim, biting the corner off his ice cream bar.

Why is it that people who are deaf to the waterfall song of a wren or blind to the overhead acrobatics of a raven can be struck dumb by the sound of cranes? I suspect it is nothing new. I imagine passing flocks drew the gaze of our earliest ancestors. Since then humans have struggled to capture the crane's voice within the narrow confines of language. The Greek word for a crane chorus is *inangling*. The Koyukon people of Alaska call sandhills *Dildoola* in mimicry of their call. Aldo Leopold described the sounds of approaching sandhills as "the tinkling of little bells," the "baying of some sweet-throated hound," and "a pandemonium of trumpets, rattles, croaks, and cries." The ornithologist Scott Weidensaul describes the sound of a far-off flock as "fingernails drawn along the teeth of several combs, but with a rich melodic sound, like delicate bamboo chimes struck with small mallets." My friend Jen says it's the ghost of an owl playing a wooden flute.

I, too, am at a loss to pin the depth of sound onto the flat page. To me the fall chorus is the sound of an irresistible smile, the corners of my mouth and threads of cranes pulled by a common force.

When my child was the size of a peanut, swimming in the warm, dark ocean of my wife's belly, we went to the doctor's office and heard that tiny heart thrumming along at one hundred and forty beats per minute. After hearing the life swelling within Anya's body, I bought a ticket to California. For years I didn't want to know where the cranes went. I didn't want to stain the magic of migration with the dangers of their destinations, didn't want to see what I knew I would find in the Central Valley. But, after hearing that little heart, I needed to weigh the chances that my child, born beneath the sounds of cranes, might live on to know a silent sky.

In Alaska, cranes bring shape and sound to the abstract notion of wildness. In California, pecking through corn stubble, the gray birds look more like pigeons on stilts. The twenty thousand sandhills flying over my home are pulled by the lingering memory of the complex wetlands that once filled the braided delta where the Sacramento and San Joaquin rivers merge in the Central Valley. The countless river channels are now counted; each one is pinned in place by high dirt levees, each island owned and managed.

I toured the levee tops with a guy named Brent, the manager of a nine-thousand-acre corn farm on the delta. Typical of farmers, Brent wore a stained, curled cowboy hat and denim jacket. Atypical was the Nature

Conservancy logo barely visible on the door of his dust-caked pickup. The Conservancy bought the farm from an aging couple who came to love the cranes that gleaned waste corn from their fields. "This is a working farm," Brent explained. "It has to pay for itself, but along the way we do what we can for the cranes." Driving the rutted levee, Brent stopped the truck alongside a group of two hundred cranes stepping through corn stubble. He watched the feeding cranes in silence. "I'm just a farmer, but you can't help but love these birds."

As with all farmers on the delta, water management is Brent's biggest struggle, too much in spring, not enough in summer. Brent showed me a stretch of steel sheet piling used to stop a leak. "This was a $600,000 patch job. You got to sell a goddamn lot of corn to make that pay." In the summer there is not enough water. An open-air aqueduct siphons the delta to quench the ever-growing thirst of millions in the Los Angeles basin. The diverted freshwater is replaced by the sea. "Not only are we below river level," Brent explained, "but we are below sea level. The flow of freshwater is the only thing keeping the sea from poisoning our fields with salt. When it comes to a pissing match between swimming pools and roosting cranes guess who's gonna lose."

We got out of the pickup and walked the river's edge. Below us, the wary cranes slowly skulked away. A speedboat careened past, heading upstream; its wake sloshed onto the dirt road. "This place is just like New Orleans," Brent said, kicking a rock into the river. "Only when the levees go it'll be cranes, corn, and a handful of farmers that get drowned out. No one even knows we're here. Don't reckon they'll notice when we're gone."

Parenthood is like having your heart racing around outside your body. Loving cranes is the same deal. I spent my last hours in California strolling along a boardwalk through a federally managed wetland. Unfamiliar passerines chirped from deep within tall grasses. Coots, shovelers, a few mallards, and an avocet paddled and poked through the man-made ponds. At the edge of the marsh, tractor-trailer rigs flashed through the leafless oaks like railroad cars with no end. Slamming car doors and faint laughter drifted from joggers doing their pre-run stretches in the parking lot.

I sat on a bench, eyes closed, facing the bright sun. A familiar twitter, barely audible above the din of I-5, snapped my attention. A slow scan of the blue sky revealed a single crane passing five hundred feet overhead. It was flying hard, trying to catch a wavering flock a few miles to the north. With luck, I'd hear the voice of this same bird winging over my home in another two months.

It takes cranes weeks to make the trip from California. In a window seat on an Alaska Airlines jet, it took me ten hours. Watching the intricate islands of the West Coast slip beneath the aluminum shell of the plane, I tried to imagine having nothing but skin between me and all that open space, the whistle of wind through feathers, the reassuring voices of mate and offspring calling behind outstretched legs.

It was quiet and snowing at home. In the following days neighbors stopped by, full of questions. I could not get through the story of our cranes living in a cornfield below sea level without laughing. Maybe being home made me giddy, or maybe it is truly absurd that the thirsty millions in the City of Angels draw water that is replaced by the sea which poisons the fields where the cranes that nest on the tundra live. Maybe laughter is like a thermal, a free ride to a view we can't reach on our own. Maybe humor is the only way to accept that staying still offers no escape when part of my heart insists on moving.

Miners carried canaries below ground because their tiny lungs gave out well before methane levels became toxic to humans; when the caged bird quit singing it was time to head for sunshine. Cranes have been called modern-day canaries; if they go, humans had best figure out why. But the canary-in-the-tunnel scenario assumes two things: the bird's vulnerability and the human's option to seek safe haven; neither assumption is a given. The resiliency echoing in the sandhill's voice since the age of dinosaurs makes them ill-suited to predict danger. The idea that humans can survive the conditions that kill off cranes remains untested.

In 1937, Aldo Leopold watched what he believed to be the last sandhill cranes to nest in his home state of Wisconsin. In response he penned his now famous Marshland Elegy:

Our appreciation of the crane grows with the slow unraveling of earthly history. His tribe, we now know, stems out of the remote Eocene. The other members of the fauna in which he originated are long since entombed within the hills. And so they live and have their being—these cranes—not in the constricted present but in the wider reaches of evolutionary time. Their annual return is the clicking of the geologic clock. The sadness discernible in some crane marshes arises, perhaps, from their once having harbored cranes. Now they stand humbled, adrift in history.

Leopold would be glad to know he was wrong, glad to know there are now twelve thousand nesting pairs in Wisconsin, glad to know the voices of a half-million sandhills still ring across the tundra each spring. After flying through eons of volcanic eruptions, asteroid strikes, and ice ages, cranes have one final trick tucked under their wide wings—inspiration.

Around the continent, from Fairbanks, Alaska, to San Antonio, New Mexico, from Baraboo, Wisconsin, to La Victoria, Cuba, people organize festivals, parades, and dances to celebrate the arrival of sandhill cranes. As the human population races to double itself in the next fifty years the fate of cranes will become increasingly entwined with our capacity for love. Alaska is big and wild, but not enough; each year over three million acres of wetlands, forest, and open space used by cranes and other migrants are lost to urban sprawl nationwide. Each year thousands of people gather alongside the remaining rivers, fields, and marshes to celebrate the sound of sandhills and say, No, not here. No more dams, no more pavement. This place is for cranes.

It is easy to kill something we don't love. Difficult to love something we don't know. Impossible to spend a fall day staring into a bowl of sky filled with wheeling cranes and not taste love.

Written in the Flesh

NITA NETTLETON

As the riot of steam roiling from the shower thins and fades in the dry morning air, I can see my image take shape in the bathroom mirror. This early in my morning routine I don't need details. All I need to know is that I am ambulatory and in one piece. Sometimes, in this gentle zone of awakening but not yet receiving the day's new information, I can review my dreams and try to reconcile them with reality. Usually it's a waste of time, as most of my dreams are not worth reviewing. They play as bloopers of any real memory or rational thought. Dreams are the responsibility of brain cells that accept no accountability for their work. When called on to report, they have a million excuses for not paying attention or taking notes. As a result, dreams often dissipate long before the steam from my morning shower does.

By the time I begin smearing protective lotion on my skin, my reflection in the mirror has become sharp and clear. As I smooth the lotion briskly over my left wrist, the surface temporarily pales and highlights a row of faint marks, cut years ago by the teeth of a handsaw blade. My skin cells, unlike those out of sight in my brain, faithfully record the events they have witnessed. Though the recordings fade over time, settling into the surrounding tissue like ripples in a pond, they do not distort. Every time I notice the saw blade marks, I remember the quick bite of pain and embarrassment exactly as I felt it years ago and get a booster shot of the lessons of fatigue and carelessness.

My face in the mirror shows in crisp detail as I dab lotion on and begin to rub it in. A fine suture runs high on my right cheek where a surgeon took great care in removing a bit of tropical sun damage barely two years ago. It is now almost invisible. I slept through the surgery, so the fading scar is my only proof that it happened. The rest of my face gets thorough attention. After I carefully dab and smooth lotion onto my eyelids, I put on glasses and take a close look at the skin over my eyes. I want to make sure my favorite scar is still there.

It was a warm May morning near the eastern boundary of Mount McKinley National Park (now Denali National Park and Preserve), and I had not brought along a jacket to wear over my short-sleeve shirt. I didn't have time to follow the meandering road, but I had more than enough for the shortcut from my cabin outside the park to the hotel's front desk where I was assigned to work for the day. I decided to explore a new route and entered the woods on an easy network of moose trails between Riley Creek and the campground. Now and then I could hear the creek's rumble in the otherwise-quiet forest. Red squirrels, ravens, and songbirds provided foreground chatter. I stopped once in a while to listen and take my bearings.

A few stops into my exploration, I glimpsed a large, unfamiliar bird. It had a hawk's head, fairly short wings with rounded tips, and it flew silently from one tree to another. Remembering work, I continued. At my next stop, I glimpsed the bird again and noticed another. The first showed two distinct shades of gray, sporting white, expressive "eyebrows." The second had mottled brown plumage, which allowed it to blend into the trees while it perched. I made mental note of both birds' sizes, shapes, and coloring so I could ask one of the birders at work to identify them for me. The instant I started walking again, I heard a piercing *key-key-key* and the brown hawk swooped over my head. I ducked, but kept going. A moment later, the gray bird dove at me as well. Shaken, I put my arms up over my head, dropped down, and scrambled under the low-hanging branches of a large white spruce. My heart was pounding. This was a new experience. Wildlife had always, always either ignored me, ambled away, or fled in terror at the sight of me. I scanned the trees and listened. My breathing was as quiet as that of the mice, squirrels, and other small creatures who know all about hiding in the forest. Both birds made another pass, zooming in fast and tipping sideways just short of the protective tangle of branches, sounding their alarm as they flew. Safe in the arms of the tree, I sat still and watched in fascination. I had no idea what to make of this situation or what to do. I was equally scared and excited. Wracking my brain for a way out without getting hurt, I realized I didn't have anything to cover my head with. No jacket, no daypack. I was wearing the white cotton shirt and a short navy blue skirt left over from my high school wardrobe, anklets, and sneakers.

Waiting for the birds to give up, for someone to rescue me, or for an idea to rescue myself, I quickly assessed and dismissed the nicks on my legs and arms from the dry branches I was crouched in. They were clearly the least of my problems. After about a minute, during which the birds did not return, I heard an alarm call fading toward the creek. I took a deep breath and duck-walked out from under the spruce branches to hustle on up the path. Not more than a few heartbeats later, the brown bird dropped silently right in front of me and smacked me in the forehead—hard enough to knock me backward onto the ground. Without thinking, I scrambled back under the tree and scooted back to sit snug against the trunk. Adrenaline washed through me. Blood throbbed in my ears. Something wet tickled my face. At the same time I saw blood dripping onto my shirt, I realized that my left eye wasn't working. I reflexively cupped a hand over the eye, felt warm liquid and then a rush of panic. I struggled to calm my breathing while I listened and watched with a new, prey-animal perspective for the birds.

Though it seemed as if every cell in my body had shifted into survival mode, my mind made room for hurt feelings. I grew up in the woods and nothing had ever hurt me. I'd hiked miles and miles through wild places. I'd taken naps in berry patches. I thought we had a deal, Nature and I. Now, serious trust had been breached. Suddenly and perhaps forever, I occupied a smaller place within the sounds, smells, and sights of the forest. I started to cry over my damaged eye and had to make myself stop because the tears stung. I did allow myself to be angry—indignant, victimized angry. If I had had a gun, I would have looked for those birds through the sights.

The river burbled, the forest went about its business, and no one came to rescue me. My adrenaline drained, rational thought returned, and I made a plan. Fresh blood had stopped running and the drying blood helped keep my eyelid closed, relieving me of the need to concentrate on it. Hands free, I broke several dead branches off the tree. I intended to hold them over my head and go back the way I had come, getting out of whatever forbidden zone I had entered. It took some courage in my newly dangerous world to leave the tree's safety, but I crawled out. I stood up and ran with the spruce branches held close to my head. I heard and saw no sign of the birds, but trotted a hundred yards or so before stopping to listen again and look back. I figured I was near the campground, so headed that way to take the road. As soon as my foot touched the roadbed, I dropped the spruce branches, reassured by the safety of civilization.

As I followed the road's serpentine twists, I couldn't help thinking about my eye, wondering how damaged it was. I held a hand over it but couldn't tell much by feel. There was no particular pain, just a general heat from the upper half of my face. Rounding a curve, I saw a young man walking toward me. I wanted him to tell me how bad my eye was. From a few paces away, I asked him to look and report, then pulled my hand away. He took a quick step back, gasped, and ran away. I stood there in shock, feeling doubly alone.

I had been abandoned first by Nature and now by my own kind.

I no longer remember getting through the hotel's bustle to the nurse's small clinic, but I do remember that she would not let me look in a mirror until she had done a lot of wiping and dabbing—first with hot water, then with alcohol—around both eyes and across my forehead. With the crusted gore removed, I was happy to be able to see out of my left eye through the swelling lid. That heady ability made the mess of the rest of my face in the mirror more a curiosity than depressing. I had no idea how scratched up I was. The hit had been high velocity by a hawk with outstretched, open talons. Evenly spaced cuts on my forehead matched single ones over each cheekbone. The diagonal gash across my left eyelid must have come from a talon closing as I began to fall backward.

Over the next couple of hours, the rumor of a bird attack buzzed around the hotel and park headquarters. In no time at all, the bird had turned into a golden eagle. Before I was sent home, a retired doctor on vacation from somewhere examined me, as did all hotel employees who could come up with an excuse to leave their posts. It was determined that the attacking birds were goshawks—one adult and one immature—and that I had ventured near an active nest. Park service staff always wore hardhats when hiking through nesting areas at the critical time.

I had been scheduled to sign up park visitors for the Tundra Wildlife Tour at the front desk that day. My supervisor winced when he saw me and told me to take a few days off. I understood. I looked too bad to be seen. As my face swelled, it hurt a little, so I took aspirin. Within hours, both eyes were blacked, shading into deep violet bruises. I didn't want my eye bandaged, so the deep diagonal scratch across the lid had to heal in motion. Hence the scarring.

I went back to work when the bruising changed from purple to yellow and used my face as a visual aid on the tour, illustrating how protective wildlife can be. I had spent my time off reading what I could find in the park library about birds of prey in general and goshawks in particular. I was glad to share what I learned. I called it a crash course, for the laughs, but added that goshawks had gotten my attention and that I would study them even more. Shortly after I'd returned to work, I rode on the bus that picked up a park ranger on his way to meet a group for a discovery hike. He had unwittingly stepped between a grizzly sow and her cub near the Toklat River that spring. The bear knocked him down and bit him on the back of his head. We surveyed each other's wounds and he talked briefly to my group about his experience.

It didn't take much time with bird books and other wildlife texts to figure out why Nature let me be terrified and injured in the woods. I hadn't done my homework. I was unprepared. I should have carried some gear with me and backed off the moment I was warned. That was the last day I hiked without things I might need. That was also the last day I used only basic guidebooks and the words of other guides for my interpretive work. I wanted to learn more and be able to answer questions more thoroughly. Learning about goshawks led to years of study and observation of other animals, and I followed the web to plants that sustain them and the ecosystems they're part of. Nature didn't abandon me at all. She slapped me in the forehead to wake me up. I consider that day in the woods along Riley Creek a most lucky misfortune.

I suffered another facial injury years after the goshawk episode. I was the park ranger this time, disposing of a can of mystery fuel some hikers had left on the Chilkoot Trail. My incineration plan was not well thought out, and though there was no damage to any part of "the resource"—which would have required massive quantities of paperwork—I flash-burned my face. Immediate dunking in the Taiya River and the trail crew's gift of a glob of aloe took care of it. As I monitored the singed, tender skin of my eyelids, I feared I had cooked off my goshawk scar. Much to my relief, it was still there when the burn healed.

Nowadays, the scar is faint and I can only see it in good light and with glasses. But I can still trace the slightly curved line all the way across my eyelid and read the story, verbatim. My skin recorded the event far better than memory alone ever could. It's like having a map as well as verbal directions, or, maybe a better analogy, having a stone tablet to go with the folklore. And the lessons in the lore are still relevant for my constantly changing life. I don't think about that day in the woods every time I smear lotion on my face, but now and then I do. Like this morning. As the steam clears and I lean close to the mirror, there it is. Today's relevance pertains to some wild turkeys I've just become fascinated with. *Don't worry*, I say back to the mirror. *I'll do my homework and give them plenty of space.*

Glad Singer

DEBBIE S. MILLER

Inside the mossy dome, a tiny orange beak catches the glow of the midnight sun. Annie and I watch closely, kneeling quietly by the stream. An American dipper chick waits patiently for a parent to return with a meal. In the middle of the streambed, the chick is tucked in the emerald green nest. This perfectly camouflaged home is woven in a misty tangle of babbling riffles, channels, cascades, and boulders. Nest and stream are one.

The illuminated beak points toward the turmoil of water that tumbles from perennial springs born deep within the Sadlerochit Mountains. An Inupiaq word, *sadlerochit* means "front mountains," as these are the first to grace the Arctic plain, the northernmost extension of Alaska's Brooks Range. My friend Annie and I are enjoying our second week of exploring this magnificent region in the Arctic National Wildlife Refuge.

Father dipper soon alights on a slippery boulder near the entrance to the nest, drenched insects dangling from his bill. We hear peeping from the chicks. All must be hoping for a share of slithery creatures. The dipper pokes his head briefly into the nest, delivering his bounty snatched from the churning stream's bottom. Then he dips, bending his knees, like a young girl might curtsy.

We watch the female dipper as she flies just above the ripples, then lands downstream on a toadstool-shaped rock. She immediately begins dipping to a steady rhythm, her head turning sideways with each bob, as though the poor bird was born with a twitch. These aren't occasional bobs—but rather forty to sixty knee bends per minute. If there were several dippers in the streambed, I'd visualize a dipper line dance: knees bending in sync, heads turning jerkily, white eyelids blinking in unison to the rushing, rapping, rollicking of the stream.

Annie and I grow fond of the dipper dance. As delirious as we already are with constant June light and two weeks of trekking across the tundra, the birds captivate and amuse us. In this lustrous world we mimic them—two six-foot women dipping and bobbing our way along the creek. We quickly determine that we can't perform the same dips without hyperextending our knees. Dipper knees bend in the opposite direction of ours. Nevertheless, we frolic and dip like silly children, laughing so hard that tears start spilling.

I first saw an American dipper as a young teen, hiking along the Merced River near Yosemite National Park. The robin-size bird caught my attention as it plunged into cascades, jounced on polished granite slabs, and trilled its merry tune. I would later read poetic descriptions of John Muir's beloved water ouzel along the Merced and other pristine rivers. In *The Mountains of California*, Muir rhapsodizes:

He is the mountain streams' own darling, the hummingbird of blooming waters, loving rocky ripple slopes and sheets of foam as a bee loves flowers, as a lark loves sunshine and meadows. Among all the mountain birds, none has cheered me so much in my lonely wanderings—none so unfailingly. For both in winter and summer he sings, sweetly, cheerily, independent alike of sunshine and of love, requiring no other inspiration than the stream on which he dwells . . .

The dipper also cheered Muir during his trip to southeast Alaska when he explored the glaciers between Mount Fairweather and the Stickeen River. While skirting icebergs in his canoe in Sum Dum Bay, he encountered the "glad singer" on a cold November day. The melodious dipper comforted him as he drifted among bergs, feeling weary and overwhelmed by the glacial landscape.

Now, nearly nine hundred miles north of those ice-choked waters, we hear the same melody alternating with the ouzels' dives and food deliveries at the nest. These dippers live on the edge of their range, where polar bears lumber along ice-clad shores.

I've always marveled at the fact that the dipper is *not* a duck, but rather the only aquatic songbird in the world, swimming, diving, and probing the streambed for its chow. But what truly stuns the mind is the thought of these same birds hunting for their supper in the depths of the Arctic winter, when subzero air temperatures are the norm.

Unlike most songbirds born here, dippers don't migrate south. As long as there is swift, open water and an abundance of aquatic insects, they are happy campers. But just how do they accomplish this in a place where they won't see the sun for more than two months?

Dippers are well suited for underwater excursions in cold climates. They grow nearly a third more feathers than other songbirds of similar size, with a large oil gland to waterproof them. Like ducks, a layer of down protects their naked skin. Tiny white feathers cover their eyelids, and specialized nasal flaps close when they dive. Best of all, they come with a cool, built-in set of swimming goggles: a nictitating membrane protects their eyes and allows them to see underwater.

Along with thicker plumage, big oil glands, and specialized diving gear, dippers also have a lower metabolism and maintain their body temperature until—ouch—it hits minus forty degrees Fahrenheit.

My friend Robert Thompson, a local Inupiaq hunter and wilderness guide, has seen and heard dippers warble in the heart of winter with temperatures hovering around fifty below zero. You'd think their toothpick legs would freeze solid and break off. But they don't, thanks to their leg structure and ability to circulate blood with minimal heat loss.

As for burning calories to keep warm, it helps having fifty to fifty-eight-degree water constantly gushing from the springs. This pulse of warm water creates an Arctic oasis, keeping the stream free of ice and meandering across the snowbound coastal plain for about five miles, even in midwinter. These birds are married to the stream, and they benefit from its warmth and year-round food supply.

Still, the thought of a sooty-gray, stubby-tailed, two-ounce bird slipping from the water into the frigid January air and *singing* to boot seems miraculous. I can buy the idea of plump penguins torpedoing through Antarctica's seas, sliding along ice sheets—but these fragile creatures? No. Cheers to another of nature's engineering feats: an evolutionary achievement accompanied by comical dancing.

In the late evening I study our wild surroundings, camped on a grassy perch, not far from the dipper nest. Just twenty miles shy of the Beaufort Sea, we have a sweeping view of the coastal plain and the mantle of thinning sea ice that curves toward the North Pole. While the future for polar bears is uncertain as the stark reality of global warming looms, there is a glimmer of hope in this vista. We can celebrate the fact that after twenty-five years of debates, hearings, battles, congressional votes, and even a presidential veto, this great land remains untrammeled, polar bears still den here, and dippers are thriving along this clean, unobstructed waterway.

Annie and I witness more scenes that could be featured on *Planet Earth*. On a stunningly transparent morning, we watch three chicks take their first steps away from the nest, teetering on slippery rocks, water foaming all around them. One by one they explore their neighborhood, rock-hopping, poking at moss-covered cobbles, and occasionally flapping their newly feathered wings. The chicks seem oblivious to us, safe in the maze of creek channels and boulders.

While watching one chick slip on an algae-covered rock, I'm reminded of our oldest daughter's first trip to the Arctic Refuge. As a one-year-old, Robin learned to walk on the spongy, flower-specked ground, the very same ground for which oil development has been proposed. She rolled and bounced across the tundra, frequently falling on the carpet of mosses and lichens. She never cried as she might have had she hit the edge of a table or chair, or belly flopped on a hardwood floor. The tundra was a forgiving mattress of plants.

Through the years our children have made many trips to the Arctic Refuge, from their toddler days to their teens. Not far from the dipper nest,

Robin and her younger sister, Casey, witnessed the migration of thousands of caribou, milling and grunting around our tent. Casey watched "boo" before she could pronounce their name. Each trip to the refuge gave them gifts of adventure and discovery, from watching wild animals and catching first fish, to finding caribou antlers, skulls, bird nests, musk ox qiviut, a new wildflower, or fossils dense with stories.

Late in the evening the magical light returns, transforming the stream corridor into a luxurious tapestry: Irish-green boulders, sparkling pearls of spray, liquid-gold riffles, and the ruby mouths of dipper chicks, wide open and begging to be fed a bedtime snack. Between foraging bouts, both parents serenade us with whimsical music: fluttering whistles, tinkling notes, and bell-like tones. If these birds played in an orchestra, they would delight us as nature's percussionists.

With temperatures dropping, the chicks navigate their way back to the nest, rock-hopping and negotiating foot-wide crossings, little wings pumping. The sun hangs thumb-high above the ocean when two chicks snuggle up in the nest. A lone adventurous one is still investigating the creek's upper reaches.

At this point the parent dippers become agitated. For the first time since our arrival, they squabble and peck at each other, feuding for some unknown reason. I guess that, regardless of species, these are just tired parents feeding three hungry mouths all day long, and perhaps worried about the fledglings' first day out of the nest. On our way to the springs, we had spotted one likely predator, a peregrine falcon patrolling a ragged cliff line. Perhaps the issue is division of labor, as nesting pairs are known to split up their brood and care for them individually. Just who *is* responsible for chick number three wandering away from the nest?

These stressed parents conjure up a horrible memory of raising our own offspring. One Saturday morning we discovered that our teenage daughter had disguised herself as propped-up pillows under her sheets. At nine a.m., we had absolutely no idea where she was, whether she was at a friend's house, had been abducted, had been in a car accident, whether some human predator had raped her, or whether she was even alive.

A missing child, and the possible loss of a child, spells the worst pain imaginable.

After a time, the lone chick gradually makes its way back to the nest and joins the others, along with the parents. All are safe and silent in their emerald hut, as purling water lulls us to sleep. Before I drift off, I wonder if these birds experience emotions similar to ours when caring for and protecting their young. What do *they* feel when one is unaccounted for?

When we sling on our backpacks, it's hard to leave these springs and the dipper family. I ponder how long dippers may have used this nest site at the periphery of a range that extends as far south as Panama. In Scotland there is a nesting site that European dippers have used for 123 consecutive years! In much of North America, dipper populations appear to be healthy and bonded to their streams, as long as those waterways stay unspoiled.

Other dippers have been less fortunate due to cattle grazing, logging, mining, similar forms of development, and pollution. I grew up in Marin County, near San Francisco, where no dippers have been sighted since 1966. In the Black Hills of South Dakota and Wyoming they are in serious decline. Colorado is monitoring dippers and lists them as a species of concern. These swimmers are unique indicators of water quality, the canary of our mountain streams.

Precious liquid continues to surge from the fractured Sadlerochits, bound for the Arctic Ocean. The watercourse and its larger ecosystem are wild and intact. There is no pollution, no industrial sprawl, no hard-rock mining, no oil development, no garbage. Like the dipper's home described by Muir in the 1800s, these Arctic streams run clear.

If Americans act wisely, this northernmost wilderness will forever be protected as a sanctuary for *life*, for all species that depend on the land and its waters: from the wandering caribou herds and struggling polar bears to the multitude of birds and one family of dippers. This is a birthplace worth saving for the world.

On the Wing, On the Plate

MARY BURNS

I t's a cold, bright, mid-November day; there was ice this morning on the narrow wooden bridge that connects Westham Island to the rest of British Columbia. I've crossed this bridge scores of times, but today it has led me to somewhere I have never been before, alongside a ditch in a farmer's field, listening to the tales of hunters.

I've devoted much of the past year to observing the Wrangell Island, Alaska, population of lesser snow geese on their wintering habitat in the Fraser Delta in southwest British Columbia and the Skagit Delta in northwest Washington State for a book on snow geese and perception. I've talked to Yupik people in Alaska, scientists in Canada, a conservation officer in Washington State, and wildlife artist Robert Bateman. But my exploration would be incomplete without the views of sport hunters.

The party I've temporarily attached myself to includes fifty-three-year-old Henry Parker, a designer of cranberry-harvesting equipment; Gil Saunier, a retired phone company employee in his early sixties; and eighty-year-old Pat Mulligan, a former conservation officer who perambulates with the help of crutches or a walking stick. The fourth member of the group is Cory May, Henry's fourteen-year-old neighbor.

A Westham Island farmer I interviewed led me to Henry, an excitable, ruddy-cheeked, black-haired, black-bearded man, who makes his own snow goose decoys and wanted to show them to me before the season began—before, he said, they got all messed up. I followed him down a narrow country lane to a barn where seventy freshly painted snow geese lay inert in their various positions, with coral red bills and feet and spots of black near the rump to simulate the folded-back primaries. It must say something about how snow geese perceive the world that these decoys can lure them into a field or down onto a marsh where hunters wait in their punts.

But that is what the three men and the boy are hoping for today. Henry set the refurbished decoys, plus about fifty others, out in this field yesterday. This morning they are moist with dew that glistens in the sunlight. If the snow geese fly over and spy a raft of shining white goose shapes, Henry claims, some will not be fooled. But as we stand and talk through the morning, the sun burns more strongly through the gauzy atmosphere, the dew evaporates, and the fake birds lose their luster. Henry, Pat, Gil, and Cory have been here since seven thirty. I arrived an hour later, and by ten we still have not seen a single snow goose.

Though I have a brother-in-law who hunts, and I lived in the Yukon Territory for several years in the seventies—when "getting a moose" was as much a part of the seasonal round as getting a Christmas tree—I've spent most of my life with city dwellers. Hanging out with Henry, Pat, Gil, and Cory, I saw that their involvement with geese is passionate, of the blood. As a volunteer for the Reifel Sanctuary, Henry has often rescued snow geese that were stranded or injured, or he's assisted the young. As a hunter, he has killed snow geese and almost been killed himself in pursuit of them. In a way that is not true of scientists—at least not the scientists I've talked to—and may or may not be true of artists, these hunters interact with snow geese on a more primal level. Until they fly north to their breeding grounds, the lyrical white birds with the ebony wing tips will continue to be engaged in almost daily battle with men like Henry, Gil, and old Pat Mulligan.

The sky is a forget-me-not blue. Pat passes around a bag of candy. We all take out our thermoses. It's after eleven and Pat is getting stiff. Henry and Gil haul him onto his feet and he leans on the cane he fashioned from a root of California bamboo.

"I want to tell you about a time many years ago down here. The foreshore was quite a bit different. There was no Reifel Sanctuary or anything. There was a good many thousands snow geese here and we got a cold spell. Now what would happen, the tide would come in, and it would be freezing cold all day long, and it would freeze the marsh, all the bulrushes—everything was covered with ice. Well, the tide would go out, but the ice would stay, and I actually saw the geese land on the outside of the ice, and then they would walk in underneath the ice and be feeding under it. Yeah. I actually saw it. They were so hungry."

"Nobody would shoot them," says Henry.

"They were no good as a table bird," Gil adds.

Many of the hunting stories I've heard feature difficulty, bad weather, and survival challenges for man and beast, and I wonder if the desire to hunt even when food can be procured by other means stems from instincts honed in our evolutionary past: the heightening of the senses in anticipation, the hard, clean feeling afterwards, of having made it through a tough experience.

The sun is nearing its zenith and Henry's dog, Tar, is bored, whimpering. The talk turns to guns, especially the one Pat uses, which, he claims, is the oldest Browning shotgun being used in North America. By now we've pretty much exhausted the possibilities of conversation related to snow geese and hunting, and it is noon; Pat has to leave for a doctor's appointment. Henry slings Pat's gear onto his back and helps the older man cross the field, the equivalent of perhaps three city blocks, to his car. We still have seen no geese and I'm wondering if there will be a hunt today. But soon after Henry returns, the wind changes; there's a taste of dampness, of salt, and Gil and Henry hear geese above the marsh, perhaps half a mile away.

It is close to one o'clock when we finally see a group of five snow geese drifting over from the sanctuary. Henry slips his camouflage jacket on and tells the dog to get down. I crouch in the grass, next to the hummock that Pat occupied for a few hours this morning. It's an odd feeling, as if I'm a kid trying to trick somebody, or a fugitive being pursued. Henry falls onto his back and fires as the geese fly overhead, but no luck—his gun jammed.

These geese have only been the advance group, however, scouting, it seems, because minutes later more geese skim our way. The hunters begin to call, "Ah, coo, ah, coo," but the geese stay far to the north, out of range. We can hear them rising off the marsh, so loud that Cory thinks they sound like a train. Henry tries calling again, "Wah, coo, wah, coo, wah, coo." Gil tries. A group of fifteen to twenty passes us high above. I tense, as if I can feel the shot about to explode, but the birds just keep gliding east.

"They got sharp eyes lookin' down at us. The bigger the bunch, the sharper the eyes. There's always an experienced one in there," Gil theorizes.

With eyes on either side of their head, snow geese have only monocular vision; they can see objects on the sides of their bodies better than those straight ahead. They also have superior distance vision and can distinguish movement. While they will ignore waving branches and grasses, they immediately spot the movement of a person or animal in their environment. But none of my research has revealed how a man appears to a goose. Images that fall upon the retina must be interpreted, and since birds need only recognize others of the same species—to reproduce—and threats to their safety, a man and a coyote might look one and the same to a snow goose, for all we know.

"The wind's picking up again," Henry observes. The mood is changing, too. Gil suggests that we hunker down in the shadows of leafless scrub willow and an old apple tree. At the sight of a skein moving in over a barn to the west, we do. This is a big group. A hundred. More? Gil, Henry, and even Cory renew their calls, all trying to imitate the sound meant to tell snow geese that there are others here: it is safe.

"They're coming right at us, Gilbert."

"Yeah, I see them. There's two bunches."

The hunters start calling again, and as the geese fly near, the voices of men mingle with the voices of geese. And then other sounds. The crunch of a shot. The thud of a snow goose hitting the ground, just across the ditch. Bang, then—thud. It's the sound that will stay with me, even though more geese will be shot in the next hour, even though it will get quite frenzied as more and more geese crowd the sky, flying directly toward the decoys.

I consider why they keep coming even as Tar splashes back across the ditch with the first snow goose I've seen shot and drops it at the foot of her master, Henry. It is a dark-gray juvenile, one of the birds that broke out of its shell in late June on Wrangel Island, Siberia (three thousand miles to the north), survived the raids of Arctic foxes, fledged in weather particularly brutal for summer in the western Arctic, then followed its parents on the traditional migration path south. Its rust-stained face shows that it quickly learned to grub on the iron oxide–rich marsh at the edge of Westham Island.

There's a real sense of urgency now.

"My way, my side!" Gil shouts, as the men start to call again.

"Here they come, over Andy's barn. Look at this, straight away! HUNDREDS OF THEM NOW!"

It looks like they're heading straight for us. The men begin to call again, but the geese never make it as far as the ditch before instinct, or whimsy, directs them back toward the sanctuary. Then another wave breaks into the cerulean band between the sea and us.

"Down the ditch! Down the ditch!" Henry signals.

This group is flying low. I know the hunters are going to shoot this time and prepare myself for another thud. I count eight shots. Three geese fall with the first four.

"I need shells," Cory shouts.

"Stay put for a minute," Henry cautions.

Excitement charges the men's voices; the calling sounds almost frantic now. As the geese come lower, I count three, four, five, six more shots. At least one goose is hit and plummets into a tree. The dog goes to fetch it, and Henry doesn't even try to stop her because the sky is literally thick with geese, an undulating sheet of black and white just overhead.

"Holy shit," says Cory. "There are so many of them."

A good percentage of the thirty-three thousand snow geese that will spend the winter in the Fraser Delta seem to have taken to the skies all at once. The air is peppery with the smell of gunpowder and homely with Tar's wet coat as she races back across the ditch with another dead goose, drops it, then races off to fetch still others from the field behind us. Alongside the first juvenile there now lie more geese, both adult and juvenile. I notice that one is still alive, and Gil immediately picks it up, turns his back to me, and dispatches it.

"It's the most humane thing to do," he explains. I think of the word *dispatch, dispatcher*: the person who sends things from one place to another, from life to death in this case, from animal to meat. The last few hours have dispatched me from imagination to reality. I see the rosé feet of the goose he just killed still swimming.

"Is it dead now?"

"Oh yeah, the nerves you know. See? Its neck is totally severed. So it'd be dead."

It's not quite two, and they don't have their limit of five birds apiece yet, but I have to make the school bell that will ring at three o'clock, back in Vancouver. Henry carries an armful of dead geese to his truck and I follow, not sure what I'm feeling. A little tired, headachey. The experience soon to be in the book, mission accomplished. If I don't know how I feel, I've learned a little of how hunters feel.

I've gathered feathers and down from the grass and stuffed them into my pocket. Now I ask Henry for a wing from one of the birds. He severs one from an adult, then one from a juvenile, and shows me where to sprinkle borax so that the decaying flesh doesn't stink. He shows me how to spread the wing and mount it. I thank him and drive away, back across the Westham Island bridge, out to the freeway that connects the country with the city. The next stage of this venture will come on the weekend, for to properly appreciate the view of the hunter and experience the geese, I feel I must eat one.

Gil suggested to Henry that I might enjoy trying a snow goose for supper, and Henry immediately thrust one of them toward me, the day of the hunt. But I couldn't imagine cutting off its head, plucking it, or reaching inside, and I was grateful that he correctly interpreted the look on my face. He actually plucked and dressed two for me and left them in farmer Robert Husband's cold room, where Robert keeps the wild fowl he harvests himself, and also, more dramatically, the carcasses of big game— deer, elk, and moose—until he butchers them.

Henry marked the bags with an A and a J so I can tell the difference between the adult and the juvenile now that they no longer have feathers to distinguish them. He warned me that they were hard to pluck without tearing the skin, and as I draw the juvenile from the plastic, back in Vancouver at my kitchen sink, I see what he means. The plucked skin is dark, not the whitish-yellow of a chicken, but browner, and torn in a few places. Yet this is a masterful job of plucking compared to what I could have managed. This bird is now as impersonal as any I've picked off of the refrigerated counters at the supermarket, except that I know this one flew a few days ago, and I know why it isn't flying any longer.

All my comparisons are with chicken because as a cook, that is the fowl with which I am most familiar. The snow geese are longer-bodied, their legs skinnier. When I saw them in the sky they seemed healthy birds, and when I saw them lying on the ground I also thought them in good shape; however, there isn't much fat on them, particularly on the juvenile. The body cavity seems larger than a chicken's, more vaulted somehow. I think of the room needed for the working muscle in a long-distance flyer—the big heart. The rib cage is composed of fine, almost delicate bones that remind me of the ribs of a carefully built ship. No wonder they appear to be sailing through the air. I stuff the cavities with a mixture of dried bread and herbs, onions, walnuts, salt, and pepper and set the oven to two hundred and fifty degrees.

At six thirty we gather at the round table in my kitchen, joining hands. We are not normally eaters of wildlife. We watch wildlife on television and through binoculars. The children join school field trips out to the Reifel Sanctuary to marvel at beautiful flocks of snow geese each October. Well intentioned, if self-conscious this evening, we mimic what aboriginal people do and thank the snow geese for giving their lives so that we can eat.

The meat is dark, tasty, not as dry as the hunters suggested it might be, and I notice little difference between the adult and the juvenile. Gil told me that, given the opportunity, he always aims for a juvenile so that he doesn't break up a pair, but also because he feels the "juvies" are a better table bird.

The power goes off for a second time that day, the result of strong winds. I run for candles.

"Now we're really living like the pioneers," I joke with the kids.

We finish all but about a quarter of the meat, and that I boil with the bones for soup. I took a picture of the carcass before it went into the soup pot, and when the bones are boiled clean I let them dry and keep them in a box on my desk so our kitten can't get to them. She has already gone wild over the wings Henry gave me, the feathers that share space with pencils and pens in a jar alongside my computer. My amulets are piling up. In addition to the bones, I have an old peanut butter jar filled with down I collected during the hunt, a poster advertising the Snow Goose Festival on Westham Island, and pictures of snow geese propped here and there. An ink-on-stone drawing of a flying, long-necked bird. Spirit stones they're called, as if spirit released from flesh could be captured in a stone. Proud notion, though it was probably just as hubristic to consider the snow goose supper a kind of communion, to think that I could grasp the lives of wild birds by swallowing their substance.

A Murder of Crows

DANIEL HENRY

The crow's writhing body throws diamonds in the rare rainforest sunlight. The bird flies crazily—twisting, twirling, hiccupping—as if warning us or clowning out a declaration of war. It careens to the buffer forest's edge and clings to a treetop where it screeches for hours. As the summer dusk gathers at midnight, the bird suddenly ceases its racket, ushering in an undertow that tugs at our dreams through the night. So ends the first day of a siege that offers new insight into the collective term for crows—murder.

False Island is forty miles north of Sitka, Alaska, as the crow flies. The camp was built at the toe of what local foresters claim was once the largest clearcut in the world. A battered swath two to ten miles wide persists across sixty miles of Chichigof Island, on the northwestern coasts of the Tongass National Forest, where towering spruce were clearcut and replaced by tightly woven thickets of devil's club and red alder. Before it became a Forest Service retreat for the young and restless in 1979, False Island was a logging camp made up of a dozen herky-jerky ATCO trailers connected by a mile of solder. Standing apart from these aluminum worm casings were a little red schoolhouse, a generator shed, a log-house sewage plant, and assorted second-thought outbuildings.

Served by a whopping road-building budget, the Forest Service built a web of roads, which allowed loggers living at False Island to haul out enough trees to supply a boggling number of upscale Japanese subdivisions. But because they still liked the sound of wind rushing through trees and the way moss-piled carpets grew deep in a mature forest, the boys kept twenty acres of old-growth "buffer" adjacent to one side of camp and called it "the woods." The woods still shelter the mouth of Clear Creek into which hundreds of salmon replay their genetic destiny every summer.

This postage-stamp forest hugs the pebbly shores of Jingleshell Cove on the Chichigof side of Peril Strait, a timid reminder of what was once an uninterrupted rainforest sprawling from northern California to the Alaska Peninsula. The squared-off patch of trees is a ghost of what struck naturalist John Muir as the tropical luxuriance he saw in the seamless woods. Nonetheless, its relative isolation and fecundity make the remnant grove a haven for animals. Shaggy brown bears still stroll and feed among fellow fauna in this hallowed space—mink, wolf, marten, deer, coyote, porcupine, birds, and fish. Look: there. A dozen bald eagles glower over the broad tide flat from the mossy, outstretched branches of the remaining seven-hundred-year-old Sitka spruce trees. There, four adult bears scoop humpies out of the creek while a sow leads a pair of cubs along a beach not sixty feet from employee quarters. Breathy explosions of killer whales prowling offshore ring among the surviving members of this token arboretum, still standing witness to the brief, reckless conquests exacted upon the neighborhood by itinerant humanity.

It is a dead-calm midsummer's afternoon when a couple of pals and I watch the first crow barrel down Main Street, squawking out its primal alarm. We are enjoying late lunch on a cable-spool picnic table outside the cook shack. On this day, most of the eighty workers in the Young Adult Conservation Corps camp are scattered throughout the Tongass on spike camps. Our ten-day missions are to build log picnic shelters and fish ladders, muck out the cross–Admiralty Island canoe trail, plant trees, or survey the inventory trails in pristine stands being readied for harvest. At the end, we will return to False Island for a few days of showers, friends, and hot grub, then light out again for the backcountry. My official title is "Group-Living Specialist," meaning that when the crews are in, I organize capture-the-flag games, film fests, kayak trips, and community gardening; when they're out, I head up whoever's left to work on camp maintenance, hustle supplies off floatplanes and barges, stir sewage, and otherwise sustain camp survival on the island's remote shores. Crows are common visitors to camp, but not like the crazy one swooping by us, screeching its apocalyptic warning.

Two sounds of the second morning stand clear in my memory. The first is of the solitary crow perched in a treetop, raucously cawing over and over in a clipped, repetitive cadence that comes to resemble the safety beep of a commercial truck backing up. The second sound is the harsh scrape of coarse feathers raking the air to interrupt our morning coffee before we could even see the squadron of a hundred crows turn a corner onto Main Street and blow past us. They scatter when they hit the trees, then join the sentinel bird in its tightly paced call. But the birds cry in different rhythms, creating a demonic clatter that builds throughout the day.

By midnight, enough crows have arrived to put one or more birds on all spruce boughs sweeping out into the camp fringe and along the beach. I hunch around a driftwood fire with friends swatting no-see-ums and appraising the shadowed crow streaks over our heads. In an hour's time, the crows' congregation assumes evolving forms: flying monkeys from *Wizard of Oz*, jet-fighter packs, insect swarms. Isabel pokes the coals with her stick. Weird, she says. A convention without joy, like a funeral. But why—who's it for? She jabs her sword in the glowing eye, then retreats into murky light and a mounting barrage.

The raucous symphony builds to a stadium roar on the third day when camp director Pete and I walk one end of the grove to the other. Tens of thousands of crows have transformed our solemn woodland asylum into a clamorous, stinking squalor. Shit flies everywhere, as do feathers and corvid epithets screamed at full volume. When we get back to camp, a visiting green-shirter from the Sitka district office asks Pete if he thinks that there's anything we should do. Pete snorts. What? Call the cavalry?

Others around camp are letting the birds get to them. Quinn takes half of her lunch break to caw loudly and throw beach pebbles at the blaring black mass in the trees. Jay Blazo (so named after he dowsed a cooking fire with half a can of Blazo white gas, then rolled away while his coworkers beat out the flames on his clothing) reports that he's acquired a headache from the ruckus. His friend Whitebird vouches for him by grimacing on demand. Whitebird is in camp recovering from an injury sustained while lighting his farts in threadbare jeans. Blazo's crew sneaked out of camp without him. They are my crew assigned to erecting a cement incinerator not far from the woods, so close-up exposure to the birds has prompted paranoia of cinematic proportions. Big Jim overhears their complaints and beams his ample, mischievous grin. He turns to show the shit-streaked barcode on the back of his jacket.

We are not alone in our preoccupation with this screeching black tide. Lone ravens and eagles perch on the periphery. A marten makes its rare appearance one morning in a bristling patch of wild celery at the forest's edge. Red-tailed hawks ride updrafts a thousand feet above the trees. Dozens of Steller's jays sit watching from the smaller trees in camp, oddly silent.

The favorite subject for breakfast discussion on the fourth day is the effect the crows are having on our sleep. One of two cooks, Michael, is as grouchy and sullen as the bald eagle we watched swoop down on a beached salmon that morning and, missing it, slam into a root wad. He says that the crows' commotion last night even drowned out a Grateful Dead jam he'd cranked up on his Walkman. Michael's scowl is a sou'easterly slamming up the ragged coast to rip away any memory of blue sky. He's drunk a gallon of coffee since getting up at four thirty; his harangue is especially honed as we trance walk within earshot. The upshot of Michael's compulsion is that his bad days are the camp's best. Our reward from his anger is a sumptuous spread—French toast in teetering columns, troughs of steaming home fries, fruit salad, link and soy sausage, and freshly squeezed grapefruit juice. Michael leans over the food, mumbling about having to eat crow to win back sleep. We nod our tacit agreement, bleary and irritated at the rising ranks of crows in the woods. The food helps. What happens after breakfast helps even more.

Big Jim is the first to leave the mess hall to face the day's work. Moments later the door opens and his shaggy blond head reappears. There's that smile again. Check it out, he says.

The rest of us, including Michael, do.

Drizzle leaks from a pregnant cloud bank scraping the treetops. There is a faint drumming on the ATCO roofs. A raven lands nearby, chuckling softly. We are swallowed in a sudden hush. The crows have vanished.

Or so we think. Closer inspection reveals thousands of muted black birds filling in the spaces of the forest like notes in a manic symphony score. Songbirds pick at berries and bugs in the clearcut tangle, gulls mew and scream over fish left on the tide flats, but the crow-ladened trees remain reticent until a few minutes before lunch.

Whitebird's face is ashen under its black bristles when he comes in for the lunchbreak. It's evil, come words between waxen lips. Consciously or not, he imitates the askew glare that Hitchcock commanded from Tippi Hedren's eyes in *The Birds*, pinned open in horror during a slashing, winged attack. Evil, he repeats. Totally outta control. We listen. Pandemonium roars from the stand of old trees. We run into the woods for a closer look.

It is a hell fight beyond our imagination.

Bodies rain from the trees. Dying birds hit the forest floor screaming like warriors startled by their final vulnerability. Their black breasts' normal gloss fades under blood and duff, pierced to the heart by beaks bearing ancient regards. We watch with grotesque fascination as silent cries issue from the twisting jaws of birds whose heads are attached to their bodies only by a strand of sinew. Many of the feathered shadows writhing on the ground are composed of two or three crows pinned to each other by their beaks and claws. Eyes hang by bloody bits of gristle. Some birds spin in silly circles as they attempt flight without one or both wings. Viscera shower us with the life essence still wriggling out of them.

We carefully pick a route from tree trunk to tree trunk to avoid being hit by the shrieking black death clusters. Despite our caution, though, we can't escape splatters of blood flying everywhere, staining crimson Rorschachs into our clothing. It is the price for satisfying our morbid curiosity, to cloak ourselves in the blood of this killing place. When I realize that in my revulsion I've stopped breathing, I turn and beeline back to camp. Leave the birds to their own dark rituals.

The mad cacophony of bird battle continues in diminishing waves until late. After a while, we hear individual death cries over the white noise of war, punctuated by kamikaze bursts of discovery and destruction. Then, in the gray of northern midnight, a feeble line of crows straggles from the grove, crossing the strait and flying away to other forests on other islands.

The victors leave us with death and ringing silence until a varied thrush breaks into burred fluting at the brightening dawn. The hush lulls me into the deepest sleep of the week, swaddled in a blanket of aural relief. Even Michael sleeps in, so breakfast comes late on the fifth day of this story. Whitebird refuses to work at the incinerator on account of vibes. I walk out with him to inspect the scene.

The few bent carcasses littering the worksite are clues, which lead us into the big trees. A palpable stench punches us as we step into spruce cover. Usually viridescent, the mossy floor is heaped with black, broken bodies. In some places the dead are piled up nearly two feet deep. We daintily pick a route through the mounds until it is impossible to move without crushing carcasses underfoot. Before long, we're kicking them like autumn leaves, raising clouds of feeding insects in our wake. Two hawks swerve in from the beach to pick through the remains. We become aware of a bloody slick accumulating on our rubber boots. Whitebird pulls back, turns, and heaves. We head back for breakfast.

Throughout the day, people sneak away to the woods to inspect the aftermath of the showdown. Isabel and Pete return with a story about a family of mink they had watched scampering among the bodies. The mother was dragging stiffened remains to her brood of youngsters who would emerge from under a deadfall to shred their gifts. Blazo claims to have watched a brown bear cuffing crow drifts like a novice golfer in a sand trap.

Big Jim nudges me awake on the morning of the sixth day. Michael is chopping onions to Creedence Clearwater in the kitchen, but no one else stirs. You gotta see this, Big Jim insists. What is it? He slits his eyes like a secret Buddha and turns toward the woods. Gotta see it for yourself.

I've reflected on that morning many times over the years. It was a humbling glimpse into the tireless life force that binds us beyond species, habitat, motivation, or income. Epiphanies such as this one come in sudden, startling, surprise packages; the shock of recognition lingers a lifetime. Whether I analyze or reexamine the event in the context of wildlife phenomena, timber practices, life cycles, or cosmic connectedness, I keep coming back to this scene.

The site of a horrific massacre has been transformed into a verdant, glowing forest floor. Even the puddles of body fluids pumped out in the crows' last mortal moments have been sopped up by the deep moss. The occasional ink-hued feather scuttering in a whispered breeze contains the only clues to the week's carnage. Big Jim and I sit, mouths open, speechless.

Gandalf the Great Gray

JO-ANN MAPSON

Shortly after I moved to Alaska from Southern California, I was driving along the Glenn Highway when I heard Canada geese calling overhead. The noise was so loud and there were so many birds that I had to pull over and watch. I poked my head out the window and studied the skein. Over a hundred birds loosely followed that distinctive V shape. Piloting on instinct, they headed south to warmer climes while I, a mere greenhorn, was about to settle in for my first winter.

I was headed into Anchorage to see the rheumatologist. The joint pains, crushing fatigue, and intermittent fever I blamed on driving the Alcan Highway in ten days with four dogs turned out to be an autoimmune disease. A blip, I thought. There was medicine to take for it. The statistics were good. I had moved here to escape the "normal" life I'd lived in California for forty-seven years. There, the wildest animals I'd encountered were roof rats that cruised the fences and occasionally got stuck in the bird feeder while scarfing down the sunflower seeds I put out for the birds.

I'd visited Alaska four times before moving. In the rural town of Palmer I'd seen ptarmigans, ravens, swans, eagles, and sandhill cranes. I put a lot of pressure on our forty-ninth state to stir things up, to breathe life into my writing, and to inspire my husband's art. My midlife plan did *not* include a jillion doctor visits, endless blood draws, tests upon tests, or the weekly injections of a chemotherapy drug that didn't make me feel any better. So one day, I up and quit the regimen. Most of the time I could pretend that I was managing just fine. When I could pretend no more, there were pills to soften the pain's edges. I foolishly thought wilderness would heal me.

Then I attended a book-launch party for *Alaska Geographic* that included a presentation of a snowy owl. Anna's Latin lineage was impressive. Class: *aves*; order: *strigiformes*; genus: *Nyctea*; species: *scandiaca*. She had come to the Bird Treatment and Learning Center with a wing injury that required amputation. She could never recover. Instead of putting her to death, one of the volunteers adopted her, and she became an "education bird," financially supported by that volunteer and on call for appearances at schools, nature centers, and fund-raisers. Disney may be able to make the owl into a jolly character, but up close and personal they are rather sinister. Those piercing eyes with the nictitating eyelids. That bone-snapping sound they make with their beaks. Serious talons are reminders of stories about people getting "footed" and having to go to a doctor to unhook the bird from their flesh. I didn't want to name her Hedwig, take her home, or claim ownership. I could see she was too wild for all that. But I wanted to be closer. To get to know her. How many birds were at that Bird Treatment and Learning place? How many were released successfully back into the wild? Volunteers who took on the task of rehabilitating birds had to be singular people. I asked one of them if I could take a tour of the facility.

Bird TLC's feathered population was made up of all kinds: a blind jay who talked like a parrot, a redpoll with a feather disorder, elderly chickadees, quails and ravens who'd gotten into some kind of disgusting goo that kept them from preening, and lots of injured eagles. Window hits, found-on-ground, emaciation, broken limbs, beak shot off by some idiot. When they couldn't be saved, broken parts were amputated. Some had infections or lice, required surgery, or needed quarantining due to pox. What should have been disgusting to me was fascinating instead. I had never wanted to be so close to anything wild in my life. I signed up to be one of their helpers. A couple days into things my joints began to argue and I tried gutting it out, but after two weeks it became clear that I had to hang up my shirt and say goodbye. I felt as if all the shining doors I'd glimpsed were shutting in front of me.

I could still appreciate things from a distance, I told myself. But whole weeks went by without me taking a hike or appreciating a view. Low-grade fevers and swollen, aching joints interfered with everything. My disease took pleasure in reminding me of my limitations and I continued to challenge it.

In the spring of 2006, I was teaching eco-criticism and environmental literature to my creative-writing graduate students. Spring is the hardest semester. The snow has melted, the world is waking up, and every living thing wants to be outdoors after being closeted all winter, especially students. Recently their eyes had begun to glaze over like doughnuts. A teacher can only do so much. What this class needed was a real live owl. An owl would make what we'd read about creatures and environmental compromise come to life. I wanted the students to decide what our responsibilities to wild creatures are, based on firsthand experience. How do you look at an injured animal versus an intact one? How do you find the hubris to decide which "rescued" animal will live and which will not? When a formerly wild bird is no longer able to fly, is it wild? How does one find the integrity in thawing out a frozen mouse, shooting it full of nutrients, and placing it at an owl's feet?

I made arrangements to have Bird TLC bring an owl to class.

Kristin arrived with a jumbo dog kennel on wheels. Tucked under her arm she carried a staff worthy of a wizard. Gandalf was a great gray, female, age three or four. In captivity, well fed and cared for, she might live to be forty. In the wild, her life span would be thirteen to fifteen years— the leading cause of death for owls there is starvation. After some jostling while Gandalf thoroughly checked us out, she settled down and perched on Kristin's fist. This was where the staff came in, as support for Kristin's arm. The tallest of the owls, Gandalf seemed enormous. But Kristin told us that she weighed only three and a half pounds. My students were rapt. I tried hard to mark the subtle cues between owl and handler, but Kristin's communication with the bird reflected a longtime relationship.

Long before we noticed any change in behavior, Kristin told us the owl was getting nervous, then made an adjustment. Every time Kristin laughed or moved her body so that the owl had to reposition herself, she looked at Kristin for cues. The students gasped when Gandalf stretched out her wings. One reached the full three feet, but the crippled wing only flared a little and folded back up. Then she fluffed her feathers, and that was the moment we all saw it: the bird's actual body beneath the plumage and talons and brilliant yellow eyes was quite small. And it reminded me that in small things, we often find our deepest lessons. Pinned down by her gaze, I realized that the owl was no less an owl for her ruined wing. Flight, I came to understand, is as much a feat of the mind as it is of the body.

A great gray owl that will never fly again trusts the perch of a woman's fist in a college classroom, and for that she may live three times her normal life span. On trash day, the ravens know exactly how much time they have to raid our garbage before the truck shows up to cart it away. There is wildness everywhere if you know how to look. On good days, when my joints allow it, I watch from the trail. On bad days I watch from the window. The spruce trees sigh in the wind and what I see passing by is no less fascinating, no less wild, no less mine.

Carried Away by Arctic Terns

ERLING FRIIS-BAASTAD

The male tern startled us when he launched himself up from the
riverbank just a few feet from where my mate and I were strolling. In
a fraction of a moment, he became a bright, white speck in the late-May
morning blue. Soon, another speck appeared; a female had joined him. As
they repeated their frenetic dance, way up and way down, between river
and sky, it didn't take more than my innate sense of a shared animal urge
to determine what was going on. The female tern was, as definitively as
James Joyce's Molly Bloom, getting in the last word. She was saying, "Yes."
She was capping an epic journey with the promise of continued life.

   In the years since I was first privileged to watch a "fish flight," as
that courting ritual is known, I have become obsessed with sleek, small,
courageous *Sterna paradisaea*. Spring after spring, I am on hand beside
the Yukon River where it enters downtown Whitehorse, Yukon's capital
and my longtime home. I begin watching for my charges to arrive in late
April, about a week before I can reasonably expect them to show up. The
gulls have dropped in from the coast by then and are making their usual
racket—an announcement of spring, to be sure, but there are too many
gulls and they are too noisy and too familiar to thrill me. At any rate,
notebook and binoculars in hand, I am there during the first week of May
when the summer's few resident Arctic terns arrive. There will be a half
dozen at most, at least until the chicks hatch, but they'll dominate my

thoughts for the next two months, well out of proportion to their number. In fact, my intrusive interest in tern doings can become downright fretful. The next twelve weeks are filled with almost ceaseless threat and challenge.

My notes tell me that in 2004 I spotted the first terns on May 7. "Water low and dirty, most gravel bars still covered by meter-thick ice. Gulls forced to the edges by it." There would be a delay again that year between the terns' arrival from the far, far south and their ability to dig a shallow nest in the gravel to house their two small, speckled eggs. As I do each year, I kept an eye on my fourteen-inch friends as they patrolled the water looking for food, crustaceans, and small fish. I admired the bright-red beaks and legs, the hip little black berets, the gentle gray wash on their backs, and the bright-white belly feathers that flash news of their approach. Again and again I'm amazed by their ability to hover in place above the river as it presents the day's choice of appetizers and entrees. I make deductions from what I can see with my own eyes and hear with my own ears, somewhat as the first *Homo sapiens* might have, back before scientists filled in the fascinating, if possibly unessential, details.

Much of what I've recorded for myself has been confirmed by my winter reading of professional naturalists. I have discovered, for instance, that terns are courageous in defense of their young out of all proportion to the parents' size. Dogs, hikers, nosy bird-watchers, gulls, ravens, and eagles—an adult tern will attack anything of any size and in any numbers. I know from my own watching that terns are loath to spend much time on the water itself, but I've watched a tern dive well below the surface, disappearing, then shoot upwards with supper in his beak.

As I go over my field notes, I'm reminded of other episodes from tern summers and speculate on what they might mean. For instance, in a couple of barely legible paragraphs from May 27, 2003, I learn that between seven and seven thirty in the evening I watched "a female on a patch of ice on the sandbar (where last summer I had spotted young)—she appeared to be being fed by two males (larger); one of them, at least, mounted her and then took off, caught a fish, and fed her immediately after, while the other male fished a few hundred yards upstream . . . Mostly." The hesitancy in those notes amuses me now. Why "appeared to be being fed" when I know she certainly was being fed? Why "one of them, at least, mounted her ..." when I know that only one mounted her? It's as if I were trying to make up for my sometimes uncomfortably strong empathy with the birds, to dilute my tendency toward anthropomorphism with a bit of misplaced, even timorous, objectivity.

I know that mere observation of the things of this world has sent many a thinker down a wrong trail. Most famously, the sun and planets do not revolve around a flat Earth. Well-polished optics and a grasp of geometry can reveal that the obvious is not obvious at all. So I read books and papers, talk to biologists, and try to maintain an open mind. A local ornithologist has told me that my local terns eat more crustaceans than fish. Not being able to spot a tiny drab invertebrate in a bird's red beak, I'll have to take his word on that. I was also told that raptors are not a serious threat here, at least to adult terns. But I have come upon an adult's body, wings and deeply forked tail splayed among the willow shoots, head and breast missing. I have watched an eagle go after young terns, and gulls harass a nesting site.

But in science, I know, it takes more than a few episodes to make a rule. Of course there would be little point to bookish study if I weren't prepared to trust experts. I learn that each year Arctic terns migrate farther than any other creature on the planet, and that they see more sunlight because they enjoy two summers, one in the far north and one in the southern polar seas. Maps festooned with arrows suggest that, after they leave the Yukon, my terns remain well out to sea as they head south along the west coasts of North, Central, and South America. However, as other arrows would have it, they may head east and then south along Europe and Africa and back to southernmost South America. Whichever route they take, that's a round trip of about twenty-four thousand miles annually. Arctic terns can live more than thirty years, raptors willing; that means a tern could cover something like seven hundred and twenty thousand miles in a lifetime. The moon is only about two hundred and thirty-eight thousand miles away! And these flyways were most likely determined by geophysical changes during the ice ages.

Miles and millennia—I marvel at the large numbers. But my attachment to the terns goes deeper. For instance, the word *tern* apparently comes to me from Old Norse, as does my name—and my genes, for that matter. I love airplanes and boats and, until recently, when awareness of my own mortality became too strong, I was a passionate angler. Now tern watching has replaced fish fighting. One June, I declared my passion on a notebook page. "The big thrill of birding for years has been spotting new species for my life list. Today, with a tern hovering only a yard from my face, I realize that these birds are a thrill each time I see them, each time I'm privileged to be close—one hovers just above my right shoulder as I write this beside the river . . ."

That leads to more dangerous thinking. Do these birds tolerate me a bit more than they used to? Are they less panicky now when I draw close? When they settle on a rock nearby, are they more likely to keep a hungry eye on the water than a wary eye on me? Have I been spending time with the same birds year after year until they think something along the lines of, "Oh, that's only Erling, a nuisance, but harmless"?

And therein lies the rub. When the angels were passing out objectivity, I was probably preoccupied with planning a life in poetry. Now, as I read over my notes, I realize that love and empathy have morphed into fretting about things I can, and likely should, do nothing about.

June 30, 2002: "At first this morning, I couldn't spot 'my terns.' There followed anxiety. Had they been disturbed? Fled? It's not yet July. They couldn't have left already. The calls of the gulls and ravens caused rushes of anxiety and resentment. I seem to empathize greatly with the struggles of the busy parents—which, by the way, never seem to take time out to play, the way the ravens and gulls seem to."

July 5, 2002: "Walked beside the river today, early—not a sign of a tern! Plenty of agitated gulls watched over by two bald eagles . . . they can't have departed already—surely after spring was so late in coming!"

June 22, 2005: "How involved to become? This morning heard squawking in the grass behind *SS Klondike*[8] . . . a large, fluffy baby bird that I had just suspected to be an Arctic tern when a parent swooped by my head. It kept doing so as I moved off. Could a raptor have dropped the youngster—too heavy to cope with that, and angry parents? Tried to reach some bird experts for an answer to my initial question." Appropriately for our short summer, they were all away from their desks.

My biggest fret nowadays is the water level. With global warming, the snowmelt in the high country is raising river levels to record heights, flooding human shoreline communities, and inundating gravel bars on which terns nest. The hydroelectric dam just above town also affects the river's height; it can be manually raised or lowered, with little warning. All that flying, twenty-four thousand miles in a year, to reproduce and keep the species going, all washed away in a flash! What to do?

If much is gained by seeing the world through the eyes of another species, some things are lost—acceptance and peace of mind, for instance—and perhaps even a piece of myself, for better or worse. A friend, knowing of my fascination with terns, once introduced me to the Naupaktomiut story "The Boy Who Became a Tern" in Howard Norman's compilation *Northern Tales: Traditional Stories of Eskimo and Indian Peoples*. Against his grandmother's advice, a youth marries an older woman. Then he ignores his father-in-law's warnings, hunts caribou in forbidden hills, and spears a proscribed spotted seal. Eventually the lad becomes a *mikutaylyuk*, an Arctic tern, and loses his human ties.

Or does he really lose anything? Perhaps the boy chooses to abandon his ill-fitting human life. The new incarnation appears more suitable to his flighty, peripatetic nature. At any rate, his life goes on—in the air, above the river, across the sea . . . Yes!

Bald Eagle

CRAIG CHILDS

I am alone, although about ten minutes ago, I could still hear voices. We intended to part for only a few minutes, each person taking a better route to our beach destination, and now we are separated. There is mud on me, smeared from crawling and pushing. Sometime today, if we keep our directions straight, we will hit the coastline. There we will regroup and tell stories about the forest behind us.

Two hundred inches of rain descend upon this island each year, sometimes two hundred and fifty. It is one of maybe a few hundred islands straggled along the west side of British Columbia. Fog hangs as if the ropes and pulleys holding the sky have snapped. The rain is a shield of gauze. Before it gets this far down, the drops are broken up, spread across broad leaves and hemlocks, and drizzled to the earth. I have been sorting through mounds of louseworts, wood nymphs, and goatsbeard. There is a documented half ton of dangling mosses and lichens in every acre of forest canopy up here. The bigleaf maples have sent roots out of their branches into the soil and epiphytes that have gathered there, sometimes a foot thick, turning the canopy, one hundred and fifty feet high, into a second root system. Fallen Sitka spruce, like massive, overlapping arms, are being digested by ferns, mushrooms, and liverworts. When I inhale, beads of water collect on the inside of my throat and lungs. I have pushed into a clearing below the locked canopy. A boggy circle is bridged by fallen trees, like the inside of a palace overgrown with foliage. Mist clings to the ground.

The sanctuary is deep with gray and green. Beards of lichens hang from the Sitka spruce. Four of the spruce are standing dead, surrounding one another, leaning in to whisper with the slow insistence of old men. I slip out of my pack and sit on a fallen tree. The seat is cushioned by several inches of wet club moss. At my feet are butterfly shapes of vanilla leaf plants and dark dabs of bead lilies. The rain must have stopped out there. Maybe it stopped three days ago. The drops are only now subsiding. The ones still falling sound like water in a cave.

I wipe my forehead with my sleeve. Above me is a ruffling sound, like a pillow being fluffed. I look up and water spatters my face. A bald eagle is perched on one of the dead limbs beneath the domed ceiling. It is shaking out its feathers and watching me with a sideways glance.

There are more eagles. Six of them, sitting in the dead Sitka, feathers puffed. The eyes are on me, inviolate stares from the head of the canopy. Another shakes out its feathers, opening a dark, robe-like wingspan, then closing it and settling. They seem to be waiting, maybe for the storm to clear, or for hunger to send them one by one back to the world. My addition is no more than someone else waiting. The eyes eventually roll off of me and concentrate on a forest that betrays focus.

Look too long at one thing in this forest, and you will never leave. All the careful maps one gathers in the glove box, all the directions to and from places showing where we are and where we have been, all are broken down in this forest. You cannot be lost here. It is a ludicrous thought that there is any way at all. I see why the people of these islands paint and carve the way that they do. Their stylized bears and dogfish, their fantastic totem poles and white-button blankets, all have the essence: hands and faces embedded into the wings of sinuous ravens, eyes hidden among the fins of killer whales. The forest is, without a doubt, eternity.

It must be an hour that we sit, the eagles and I, before I hear voices again. People have found one another. I can hear laughing. The shore must be close, and they have found some route. The voices draw me off the fallen tree. I shoulder my pack. The eagles are unmoving in their shrine, feathers rolled out.

Later, we are near the village, on the beach. Someone has a crab and a pot of boiling water. We have to tear the crab apart while it is still alive and stuff it into the pot because the creature won't fit whole. The first thought is that this is inhuman. Then I imagine an eagle jerking apart the fine, strange organs beneath the crab's carapace, while the crab vainly struggles. We are cracking red shells, drawing out the white, fresh meat. What happens next is that a bald eagle appears from the dark of the canopy and flies over the shore. We can hear the deep thump of its wings, and suddenly I jump and run after it. One account is that I'm running in circles with my hands to the sky. Another is that the crab has suddenly made me ill.

What I had seen was one of the round black feathers loosen from the inside of the eagle's wing. It is a short, dark feather with white down at the base, the kind that cups air, holding the bird to the sky. I run after it, following it through the ripples the eagle has left behind. The feather drifts over the sea, and I run into the water. I am running as if the sky has just caught fire and I am trying to catch the very first ember. The feather comes back to land and I am beneath it, with cupped hands.

It settles in my open palms, gentle as something that is not even there. I bring it to my chest so a breeze will not steal it. I unfold fingers and look into the hollow formed there as if I have taken hold of a piece of flight and of wildness itself.

When I look over at all the crab eaters, they are staring blankly at me. I grin and gesture with my hands that I have caught the feather. They force strange smiles with meat in their mouths and gesture back with their crab legs.

FINS, FLUKES & FLIPPERS

First Salmon

KAYLENE JOHNSON

*E*ven *before the electrical impulse, before the spark of life created*
movement—before a flick of tail or fin—her eyes stared beyond the
membrane of her embryonic cocoon. She saw the graveled texture of her redd,
a cradle created by her mother in the bed of a freshwater stream. She saw
gradations of light as the long days of summer moved toward winter. She saw
shadows: a moose's dark hoof as it narrowly missed her bed, a bear's paw
swiping by, the silhouette of eagles' wings passing overhead. And she saw the
mottled shapes of adult salmon moving laboriously through cold water. Birth
and death happened simultaneously here in the hushed eddy of this quiet stream.
But she could not know this, as knowing goes, the primordial cycle of life and
death. She could only see with eyes around whose forms a body slowly grew.

In late winter, the stream's pristine waters maintained a steady temperature
under a thin slice of ice that closed the river to predators and other hazards.
On top of the ice lay three feet of snow. Underneath, a translucent head as
well as a slender body and tail emerged from the salmon's bright-orange egg
sac. She could move now, but only in flickers, as she and her alevin siblings
grew crowded under their protective gravel sheath. Still, the most prominent
features of her body were golden eyes, huge and unblinking, which absorbed
the very essence of this place. Somehow she would remember it all, assimilate
every detail about these waters, the scent of the seasons, the colors of rock and
snow and sky. Although her body fed on the ever-shrinking yolk, something

beyond the fullness of these nurtured days of growth began to stir in her cells. Something akin to longing.

The gray of winter dissolved into the brilliant sparkle of spring as lengthening daylight melted the snow and ice. In a desperate press against the confines of her watery womb, the salmon—barely the length of a human fingertip— dislodged first one, and then another, pebble. The current, made stronger by snowmelt and rain, gently pried the rest of the redd apart. Suddenly she found herself swept up and away by rushing water. Instinctively, she shuddered and flexed, then swam. Yet her strength was nothing against the power of water, and she tumbled downstream until the current deposited her into a shallow back-eddy several yards from where she had hatched. Her tiny gills heaved with the free-falling sensation of a universe breaking open, beckoning. She was, for the first time, hungry.

Our four-year-old son, Erik, suffered one frustration after the other, trying to catch the bountiful and yet elusive salmon. Our family had watched from the viewing deck of Ship Creek as salmon leapt Herculean heights against the current to clear a waterfall that blocked their upstream passage. Again and again, the salmon threw themselves against the white water, and inwardly I cheered each time one of them cleared the falls. Their journey home seemed both noble and incomprehensibly difficult. They had traveled far into a wide ocean-world. And yet here they were, willing to dash themselves against raging falls to return to the small stream or eddy where they first hatched. I remembered how Alaska had felt like home from the very first moments our family arrived here a few short years earlier and wondered to what extent migration was a part of my own life. While I considered the moves of body and soul, Erik thought of only one thing: he wanted to catch a fish.

Ship Creek was closed to fishing, so we decided to try our luck at one of the most popular spots along the Russian River. Sockeye salmon choked the stream where fishermen were known to stand shoulder to shoulder in a stance known as combat fishing. It was our first try. The season opened at noon, and knowing how popular the fishing hole was, we came early and parked along a grassy curve in the river. Slowly, more fishermen began to filter in, and as the clock's hands moved toward noon, Erik positioned himself on a tuft of shoreline protruding from the bank. Just moments before the appointed time, a man in waders stepped in front of Erik, making it impossible for him to cast his fly into the water. Another man joined the first, and soon a wall of fishermen blocked any shore-side access to the river.

I was incensed. "How rude," I said. "Can't you give a little boy room to cast?" With averted eyes, the fishermen ignored us.

While I fumed over Erik's dilemma, the noon opening began. The river became a boil of salmon as fish fought at the end of dozens of lines that had dropped simultaneously. Fishermen called, "Fish on," a warning for neighboring anglers to pull their lines from the water until the salmon could be landed.

After two hours of waiting with anticipation, and now standing three feet behind the chaotic action, Erik started to beg. Couldn't we please carry him, just hold him as we stood in the water with our own waders while he cast his line?

Meanwhile, his two-year-old brother, Mark, leaned over the bank's edge, grabbing for smolt that darted through icy waters. As we tried to comfort Erik and come up with a new plan, Mark overreached and, with a splash, toppled into the river.

My husband, Todd, retrieving our wailing toddler by the scruff of his lifejacket, said, "This just isn't going to work."

I agreed. "Let's go."

Erik buried his face in my shoulder and wept.

She spent her summer days foraging, picking at plankton and anything else that might nourish her ravenous growth. Between the hours and days of continuous browsing came spasms of panic as predators feasted on the fry. Eagles and seagulls regularly scooped fingerlings into their craws. Ducks and a family of young otters fed on the tender fish. Somehow, with skittish luck, she managed to flash past probing beaks and snapping teeth.

Later in the summer, piscine freighters moved into the stream, and she knew to stay out of the way as adult salmon began their spawning rituals.

Females riffled their tails through the gravel, creating nests for their young. Males fought each other for the opportunity to lay milt upon the eggs. The adults' stately movements were tinged with deep fatigue. Many of the older fish were already fading in color as the life force leeched from their bodies. After spawning, they deteriorated even further. Chunks of graying flesh hung from their washed-out forms.

But the smolt grew bolder. Something about the scent of older fish drew her closer, something familiar yet strange. A spawned-out salmon lay on its side. Its tail waved feebly and only occasionally—just enough to keep it from turning completely belly up. She approached the dying fish and on impulse nuzzled a gash in its back. Obeying a mysterious and ancient dictum, she then opened her mouth and began to feast.

Back at our Russian River camp, I changed Mark into dry clothes and wiped Erik's red-rimmed eyes and runny nose. Todd broke down the fishing rods while I made sandwiches at the picnic table.

I could not recall when I had been so angry with strangers. Wasn't fishing a way to connect with earth's bounty, an opportunity to reflect on the natural rhythms of life? Wasn't catching that very first fish a rite of passage, an initiation they too had enjoyed as children? Yet these people behaved as though they might not survive the coming winter if they did not haul in a truckload of salmon. Judging by the fish churning this river, weren't there enough for everyone?

I later learned that while a hundred and fifty million wild salmon return each year to Alaska's waters, the Russian River is one of only a handful of in-state salmon streams accessible without a boat or small aircraft—so fishermen without these expensive accoutrements flock to it like hungry gulls.

As I cut the boys' sandwiches into halves, a tall, white-haired man approached, wondering if we might loan him a fingernail clipper.

"Sure," Todd said, reaching into his pocket.

"Would you mind clipping the line from this fly?" he asked.

He turned his head to show us a one-and-a-half-inch fishhook imbedded in the cartilage of his ear. A string of fishing line hung from the hook's eyelet.

"That line—it's bothering me something awful," he said.

Horrified, Todd snipped the line and asked if he needed a ride to the emergency room.

This man had also just been at the Russian River fishing shoulder-to-elbow with others. A woman next to him cast her line, accidentally hooking him in the ear. Rather than offer an apology, she had clipped the line, tied on another fly, and continued to fish.

"I think I've had about enough fishing in this place," he said.

We nodded. This wasn't fishing. This was madness.

After growing sleek and silvery, something in her cells told her it was time to leave this place. So she, along with what remained of her siblings, slipped downstream toward a vastness they could not comprehend, toward saline waters that had called and sheltered generations of their forebears. Yet she and the others did not travel headlong toward the ocean. Instead, they allowed the current to push them tail first downstream. As the water swept her toward her future, she looked with lidless eyes at the place of departure. And she remembered.

In the ocean, she joined other salmon her age and size. Here, the dangers were just as numerous as in the stream of her birth. But she moved freely now, not bound by narrow banks. She traveled in a school that flashed its shiny flank like one enormous organism. Whales, sharks, seals, dolphins, and sea lions preyed on it, taking their fill but still leaving bountiful numbers for the next predator. In these waters she grew strong and muscular. Her flesh deepened to a rich shade of red as her body readied itself for a long sojourn. Her scales shimmered like a polished coat of armor. The ocean's munificence fortified her, and she grew larger than her freshwater home would have allowed. As one and then another year passed, she learned the sea's dangers. She might have been content to stay put indefinitely, except that, as seasons turned, the memory of freshwater began to pull at her. Egg follicles formed inside of her and with them, desire. Earth and water directed her; the low voltage of the planet's magnetic aura and the moon's sway over the tides stirred her. Finally, as she and her kin traveled closer to shore, she caught a scent that propelled her forward: the scent of home.

Later that summer, we heard about a small, salmon-rich slough off the Knik River. Retreating tides lowered the water level, creating elongated pools along the mouth of the river. Salmon swam circles in these watery pens, locked in by sand and gravel until the next tide reopened the river's corridors. It seemed like a perfect place for a little boy to catch a fish.

We arrived late in the day, at low tide, determined to stay as long as Erik wanted to. The summer sun accommodated our plans. At that time of year, after a rosy midnight sunset, the pale glow travels just below the horizon across the northern sky until it pops up again as a fiery ball over the eastern mountains

Erik cast his pixie into the pool. The spoon lure sparkled through clear water as he slowly reeled it back to shore. He cast over and over, with the ease of someone who had been born to fish. He fished with resolve, trying different pixies, casting from different positions around the pool. But no matter what he tried, the salmon were indifferent to his hook. Todd helped him to change lures and untangled the occasional nest of fishing line in the reel.

Mark had long since grown bored, so he and I scouted the riverbed for other treasures—rocks, seaweed, and muddy puddles to jump in. Even I was growing restless while Erik and Todd exhausted all venues of catching salmon.

As the evening got cooler, I marveled at Erik's determination. His intensity seemed to reflect the migration of salmon itself. I suspected that somehow, in some ancient but now-latent genetic code, humans had been wired to harvest rivers. Erik, at least, seemed to have tapped into some primal and insistent aspect of his nature.

"Mom," he called. "Could you come here?"

"Sure," I said.

"Here," he said, pointing at the muddy ground. "Right here."

I kneeled next to him wondering what he had in mind. Still casting what was now a pink pixie, he sidled up to me and leaned heavily against my shoulder.

"What do you need, Erik?" I asked.

Erik sighed deeply. "I need you to hold me up," he said.

Too tired even to stand, he refused to give up his quest for salmon. Only with firm and solemn promises that we would soon return did we convince him that, perhaps, it was time to go home.

In estuary waters her desire grew pressing. She stopped feeding. Drawing on memory ingrained in her DNA, she knew she had been here before. And she knew where she was headed. As she muscled upstream against the current, water washed through her gills in a rush of oxygen and urgency. All she had seen on her backsliding journey to the ocean now rematerialized. She charged into the sprinting water, leapt over rocks, dove under fallen trees. As eggs swelled in her body, her urgency became a sort of rage, an aggression that dared the very stars to keep her from reaching her destination.

As she expended stored supplies of fat, as hormones and enzymes surged through her blood, her body transformed. Her flesh paled while her scales turned the color of fireweed in fall, an unrelenting flame. Her head changed from a smooth, stretched-out U to an angry and angular V. She appeared formidable, yet not nearly as fierce-looking as her male cohorts, who sprouted jagged teeth along hooked jaw lines. Like her, they drove forward, but not before shimmying against her, testing to see if the time for courtship had arrived. Although the home scent grew stronger, she was not content in any waters except those lodged in her memory since the moment of conception.

Finally—battered and bruised by miles of upstream struggle—she arrived. With great deliberation, she dug her redd, accepted a mate, and then released eggs into the gravel bed. The last of the fury that had propelled her was spent. The kinder waters of the eddy soothed her. Her battle was over and she could rest.

The summer after Erik failed to catch his first salmon we tried again, this time along the banks of the Little Susitna River. We camped on an island, cradled by stream channels, at a place where we could cast our lines with minimal interference from rapacious fishermen. Erik flung his lures even as we set up our tent. Mark climbed an alder tree, trying to entice his brother to join in the fun. Erik ignored him.

I watched my son's intent and focus, his movements fluid as water. A year had passed since his last attempt to catch a salmon, and both boys now were an inch taller.

Eventually, we convinced Erik to eat and come to bed. We had the whole weekend to fish. In the middle of the night, we woke to the patter of rain on the tent. Slowly, it grew louder and more insistent, until sheets of rain pelted the flapping nylon. By two a.m., water began to seep through the seams of the floor. By three a.m., our sleeping bags lay in cold, muddy puddles. We worried more about access back to shore than we did about the dripping tent. To get to the island, we had walked in hip waders, carrying the boys piggyback across a twenty-foot channel. As more rain fell the water rose, and we feared we might need a boat to get off the island.

The next morning, with rain still lashing the water and the river rising, we packed up and began hauling our gear back to the mainland and up the mile-long trail to the car. This time, we nearly swamped our waders. Perched on our backs, the kids had to lift their feet to keep their boots dry.

Erik's disappointment was cavernous. Hadn't we promised he could fish the next morning? He hadn't caught a single salmon. Not last summer. Not this summer. Not one.

After crossing, Erik pleaded to fish from shore while we carried our gear to the car. A middle-aged couple that stood several yards downstream from where we had crossed assured us they would keep an eye on Erik if he wanted to fish for a while. We agreed and strapped a life vest to his slender frame. Perhaps twenty minutes of casting would lessen his frustration at leaving the salmon behind.

The current now was slow-moving, clear mountain water. From behind rocks, smolt appeared. Tentative at first, they became more intrepid at her sluggishness. Her body had grown so heavy, almost too cumbersome to move. All that remained of her will had shriveled into the slow, occasional swish of her tail. Eventually even that grew tiresome, and she lay limp, sideways, suspended in the shallows. The only life left glimmered from her eyes, the same eyes that had first registered light and shadow here. Motionless, she watched.As still as she had been in the beginning, she absorbed the swirling, took in the colors of rock and sky—and watched as a new generation fed on her flesh.

The cry of a seagull pierced the evening air. And downstream, a little boy fished, hoping that maybe this time he'd finally catch one.

When we returned from our second load to the car with Mark in tow, Erik met us with wide eyes and a breathless smile.

"I got one!" he said.

"No!" I answered.

"Yup. It's right there, in the grass."

Todd and I looked at each other and then at the couple whose grins reflected Erik's joyful surprise. Sure enough—in the tall green grass there lay a large chum salmon.

"Your boy did a great job," the man from downstream said. "He kept the rod tip up and held the line tight until I could get to it with my net. It's the only fish I've seen caught all day."

I couldn't believe I'd missed it—missed the sight of Erik's face as the force of twelve pounds detonated against his line. How his young arms must have pumped the rod and flown at the reel with the salmon's lurching and diving. I felt my throat constrict. My sons had become the port at which I'd anchored my deepest sense of purpose. Was it possible that, already, Erik was embarking on a migration of his own? That this was just the beginning of a long and tender leave-taking?

Erik slid his fingers under the salmon's blood-red gills and hefted it up for us to see. Held chest-high, the salmon nearly eclipsed his five-year-old body. The sleek fish glistened like chrome. Bands of green and purple striped its sides. Erik could only hold it up for a few seconds before dropping it back onto the damp grass.

With arching gestures, my son described his battle with the salmon, how it had almost pulled him into the river, and how it had struggled first up- and then downstream before he managed to reel it in. Squatting next to his prize, he slowly smoothed his hand across the cool wet scales. Quietly, with a hint of reverence, he said, "This is a very fine fish."

Certainly I could not argue with the fine-ness of this moment.

It has been said that the story of migration is the story of promise—the promise to return. I hope this Alaska wilderness and memories of our family will imprint my sons with direction and purpose. I hope that, no matter how far they will wander, they can return to those memories for guidance, for a sense of belonging.

Looking Over the Edge

MARYBETH HOLLEMAN

We are standing on the edge again. We've walked through fields of lupine that seem lit from within by a luminous mist gilding their purple pouches. Now we peer over a cliff, looking for the wildlife that clings to the rim of St. Paul Island in summer. A puffin wings by below, its back shining through gauzy fog, its head tilted to look up at me without dropping a single one of the half-dozen silver fish in its multi-colored beak.

Here at Zapadni Point are birds I have seen before, but never in such a dramatic seascape, and never in such numbers and variety: horned and tufted puffins, black-legged and red-legged kittiwakes, crested and rhinoceros and lesser auklets, cormorants, and murres. Hundreds, thousands, cluster together, pressed to vertical rock, where, amazingly, they lay their eggs and raise their chicks.

The Pribilof Islands—St. Paul and its sister island St. George, fifty ocean miles south—float like emerald life rafts in the middle of the tumultuous Bering Sea. At three hundred miles from the North American mainland and five hundred miles from Siberia, these bird roosts are about as far away from anything as you can get, even for those like me who make their home in Alaska. Remoteness paired with notorious wind, waves, and fog limits human visitors to only a few hundred per year. But for multitudes of wildlife, the islands are in exactly the right place. They are in the middle of everything—if your diet is northern marine—and lifesavers if you're blown off course from Asia or Europe or North America.

The Pribilofs have long been renowned for the incredible confluence of wildlife that returns each breeding season. They are unique not just because of the birds, though that would be more than enough. Their other dominant summer resident is the northern fur seal. Both volcanic islands, a mere eighty square miles of conical hills and tundra, meet the sea with soaring cliffs just right for nesting seabirds, and they have beaches and promontories perfect for fur seals to breed, give birth, and raise pups. Between them, they have traditionally harbored 80 percent of the world's northern fur seals.

Those seals. The ones we hear and smell on the far side of the highest hummock. The bellows, the squeals, the barks of an entire community of fur seals at Zapadni Rookery.

Evening finds us on the outskirts of the Reef Rookery. My husband, son, and I accompany a small band of wildlife watchers, visitors from as far away as Germany and as close as Anchorage. Both my husband and I have lived in Alaska nearly a quarter of a century; my son knows no other home. But all of us, no matter how far we've traveled or how well we think we know Alaska, are as agog as if we'd just arrived on another planet.

The Reef Rookery is closest to the town of St. Paul, or what one hand-drawn local map refers to as the human rookery. The huddle of a few hundred people is nothing compared to the aggregations of fur seals and birds. It's a relief to see that human rookeries have not overrun wild ones. This sense of proper scale is, however, illusory. Sometimes, when you peer over the edge, you don't see everything.

In this treeless landscape, I can see the rookery from a distance. Looking down across green hills, I quickly take in its stratification, as clearly marked as intertidal zones. Nearest the surf, among a bouldered shore, are tight groupings of dark pups with bobbing heads and large liquid eyes. Clustered nearby are looser groups of lighter-colored females. In between these gatherings, a massive, thick-necked bull stands out—the harem master. Above the harems, farther up the beach, the seals spread out, no longer in groups, but in individual territories.

Between the harems and us, a path snakes to a viewing blind, a wooden platform with openings in the sides to safely watch fur seals. The seals, however, are not just below the blind; they are in the fields surrounding it. One large young bull is even lying in the middle of the path before us.

Most wildlife sitting on a trail I am traveling will dash away, disappearing almost before I know what I've seen. That's how I have come closest to lynx, coyote, wolf, bear, and fox. Marine mammals do the same thing when they are in water. On land, where they cannot move as fast, they rarely stray from the water's edge. The pinnipeds I'm familiar with—mostly Steller's sea lions and harbor seals—stay put until a person reaches some critical point, at which they will slip away to wet safety. These fur seals, though, are hauled-out at least a ten-minute scooch from the ocean.

Distance, however, is not the problem. It's rather those six-hundred-pound harem masters lining the shore. They will terrorize in a most bloody fashion any male that dares trespass through their bevy of females. The adolescent bulls' biggest problem is that they cannot safely get back to the sea.

I witness an attempt later that night, when my husband, Rick, and I return to Reef Rookery. A single male starts toward the water, but as soon as he enters the harem zone, a half-dozen older bulls charge toward him, then begin biting and growling and pushing him around. He tries valiantly to find alternate paths to the sea, but the bulls do not let up. Instead, the brutality intensifies so that I can barely stand to watch. Bleeding and battered, the young bull finally retreats.

As for the three-hundred-pound fur seal now on our path to the blind—where can he go to get out of our way? Dozens of other young bulls rest evenly spaced across the grass all around us. To move would mean crossing onto another seal's turf and risk a fight. Often, the seal simply won't budge, and people have to turn back.

I have seen this intransigence before with other wild animals, especially very large and stubborn moose. I try to remember that we are visitors on their home turf; in a standoff, we are the ones who should back down. Our guide Dylan explains the need to yield differently: these seals are dangerous. Hidden in tall grass or camouflaged among boulders, fur seals have attacked people. "One bite can sever an artery," he says.

Fortunately for us, this one decides to leave. He slide-jumps across the gravel faster than any seal I have ever seen. Despite their awkward gait, fur seals move surprisingly far inland, farther than any pinniped. The Staraya Artil Rookery on St. George, for example, perches more than two hundred feet up a grassy slope. It's an odd sight, marine mammals so far from the sea.

With the seal out of the way, we walk single file to the blind and up three wooden steps. Weathered gray and stippled with pale-green lichen, the blind looks as if it could crumple to the ground any moment, like it's been standing here for a hundred years, rather than a couple of decades—a testament to frequent winter storms with high-breaking seas and winds above eighty miles an hour. But that turbulence, together with the cold, rich current pouring north from the Aleutian Basin, creates prime feeding grounds for seals and seabirds. Here, with violence comes fertility.

My son, James, takes the lead and strides to one end of the oblong platform. Startled by a sudden loud sound, something in between a snort and a bellow, he jumps back. A large male reclines on rocks just outside the blind, so close that we could, if we had one, drop a fish into his mouth. Instead, we all inch toward the blind's edge and take turns peering through one of two openings at the agitated beast.

There's nothing endearing about the face that stares back at me: large blood-shot eyes, rounded in fright masking as bravado; short, blunt snout; teeth exceedingly pointed and sharp. It's easy to imagine how those interlocking teeth tear into pollock or squid; easy to imagine how they inflict upon other fur seals the type of gashes visible on so many. This bull is big enough to be a contender for harem master. He might already have tried, judging by the wounds and scars that riddle his body.

Meanwhile, at the other end of the blind, Bob—an attorney with a booming voice—and James are watching, and apparently irritating, another large male. He snorts and spits, shaking his massive head, making the blubber on his neck and shoulders ripple.

Both of these seals react more strongly to Bob and James than they do to the rest of us. I can't help but wonder if this is because James is an adolescent male and because Bob is boisterous and assertive. Do the seals feel more threatened by them, or challenged?

The fur seal's wiry whiskers poke through the blind as he grunts another warning to my son. "Step back, James," I say at the same time as Dylan says, "Don't stick your hand through there, they'll bite." Rick laughs. "Isn't that obvious?" he says. But Dylan just smiles and replies, "You'd be surprised how many people need to hear that."

Though I have heard that northern fur seals are particularly aggressive, I'm still stunned by just how menacing they act. I've spent some time around sea lions and harbor seals, including boating and kayaking in southeast and southcentral Alaska, hiking out to remote rookeries and haul-outs, and even swimming with sea lions in the Galapagos Islands. Sea lions can be bullies when they defend salmon or breeding females. Harbor seals rarely are.

Without doubt, these fur seals are different from everything I've experienced. They are much more aggressive and territorial toward us and toward each other. It makes me almost dislike them. For an avowed wildlife addict like myself, the feeling is unsettling.

Perhaps, however, that very same ferocity has saved them, at least so far.

A history of exploitation haunts these fur seals, so much so that it's a wonder they have not followed Steller's sea cow into oblivion. Despite the appearance of plentitude, this stunning assembly is vulnerable. Put all your fur seals on two small islands, and you can quickly run into trouble.

These are my thoughts as I stand on a hill overlooking the Northeast Point Rookery the next evening. The world's largest fur-seal rookery, the greatest concentration of marine mammals ever, endures—but greatly reduced. A mere fifty years ago, these two islands sheltered 2.2 million seals. Today, around eight hundred thousand are left.

This slump in population is not unprecedented. Twice in the past—in the early 1700s and the early 1900s—sealers slaughtered so many animals that their numbers fell far below today's count. Behind us on the hill stands a stone memorial to a sailor who fought seal pirates. In the early 1900s, after open-sea sealing was curtailed, foreign poachers would come ashore under the cover of fog to take seals. Aleuts, deported to the Pribilofs by Russian fur traders to kill and skin seals, battled against these pirates.

The days of seal pirates and commercial sealing are long over; the current population decline is related to lack of food. Overharvesting (both from today's intensive pollock fishery and whaling a half century ago), global warming, sea-chemistry changes, and a host of other factors also are suspect.

I knew all this before I came to the islands. I had researched and written about the faltering Bering Sea ecosystem; I spent long hours talking with friends who grew up on the Pribilofs, who remember how busy with seals these shores once were. But the visceral presence of loss still astonishes and saddens me.

From this hill I can see where all the seals used to be. The land retains their shadowy outlines. Where now roughly a thousand seals sprawl, hundreds of thousands once blanketed the grass. The outlines are brown ground on which grass has not grown again but holds back, lest the missing seals return.

After two days tagging along with Dylan's group, the three of us veer off, having arranged our own viewing permit for the rookery blinds. I hope that, faced with fewer people, the seals will be less defensive and fierce.

We try the blind at Zapadni Point first. It sits above a haul-out for seals that are either too young or too old to breed. If they are not defending or trying to usurp harems, then perhaps they will be more tolerant. A low, rocky shoreline topped with the blind flanks one side of the beach's sandy curve. A steep cliff marks the other where the haul-out gives way to bird rookeries. Inland from the foreshore, a seal-trampled meadow resembles fields of cut hay.

The seals lie fanned out, not tightly bunched as in harems. Young seals cavort and tumble across the sand, until such frivolity is quashed when they venture too close to an older, and larger, seal. I cannot tell whether they are playing or fighting, but the skirmishes look harmless in comparison with what we've seen before, and they don't result in noticeable injuries.

To my surprise, a couple of Arctic foxes skitter around boulders and seals, their searing amber eyes trained on us. They are one-tenth the size of even the smallest of seals, but neither species pays the other much attention. When we approach the beach, however, everything changes. Like a single organism, the seals turn toward us and glower. Some of them roar. Some shake their heads, blubber joggling. Some even fake charge.

It reminds me of the movie scene where the bad guy walks into a bar, and all conversation stops as heads turn to stare down the intruder. As long as we stay in the truck or the blind, they mostly ignore us. Visible, we're the bad guys.

Back in the Reef Rookery blind on our last day, James is trying to get a close-up photo of one male's face. The seal is spitting, baring his knife-edge teeth, and rolling his eyes, showing their whites; he is craning so fiercely that I expect his head to rotate all the way around. Then he stretches his neck like a seamless accordion and aims for James's hand on the camera. "Stand up!" I yell. James stands and points his camera down at the seal. The seal wedges his snout between the lowest board and the floor, reaching for James's leg. He's not kidding. He wants us to leave him alone.

But this time, I can see more than just viciousness in the snarling, fanged face. I see the tenacity it takes to survive in a place marred by violence both human and natural. And I see something beyond even the requisites of survival.

At Zapadni Point, along the cliffs at Southwest Point, and past the breakers at North Beach, I observed fur seals in the water. They glided down wave fronts like bodysurfers. They lolled on the surface of still water, raising one hairless flipper like a sail, boneless tips flapping. They floated with backs and heads curved, a pose for aquatic yogis. A pair frolicked in a rocky tide pool, taking turns entering and chasing each other out, flipping over and splashing for no conceivable reason other than pure pleasure. They leapt out of the water, sometimes becoming entirely airborne. They arced through the sea, looping around each other in such harmony, with such ease, that I could hardly believe these were the same beasts that tore at each other so mercilessly.

Perhaps they responded to the safety of water, its expansiveness. They spend most of the year, most of their lives, out at sea, with all the room in the world. The rookeries must seem like jail, so confining, so crowded— and so dangerous. They can move relatively quickly on land, but not nearly as quickly as in water. No wonder they are so ornery on shore.

The power of edges is sublime: where you stand determines what you see. At the edges, grace and violence intermingle. As I stand in the weathered blind, watching a scarred harem master point his snout at the sky and small pups with wobbly heads bleat for milk, I am humbled once more by the riches of this Alaska, by the lessons it keeps giving, and the ways it continues to astonish. I came here wanting to immerse myself in wondrous plenitude; I had not wanted to face brutality or loss. But a fur seal's ferocious face reminded me how one cannot exist separate from the other—how I can bask in beauty only because there is also the terrible knowledge that this, too, is as fragile as a lupine's jeweled bloom.

Prince William Sound Herring

MARIA FINN

A man in the Lower 48 asked me if the following story could be true: A friend of his had visited a Native village along the Yukon River. At that time, salmon bones were falling from the sky like manna from a cantankerous god. Fish skeletons littered dirt roads and boardwalks. Only those who had spotted tail feathers vanishing into the trees, or beaks aimed for the streams, were privy to the mystery's origin.

I had never spent much time in Alaska's interior and could not answer his question, so I told him my Galena Bay story instead. In the spring of 1991—after the *Exxon Valdez* spilled oil into Prince William Sound but before that pollution took its lasting toll on the herring migration—I worked with another deckhand on a small aluminum jitney, tucked away in one of the sound's many coves. It was only my second season of fishing commercially. Although I was in my early twenties, I had never in my life caught a fish on a pole. My fellow crewmember Kimberly had worked her way around the world by turns as a skier, scuba diver, and fashion designer. On that day, both of us were waiting for the herring to arrive. Our skipper, Jackie, was off in some other bay, flirting with the fishermen of the fleet, most likely on a fifty-two-foot seine boat with an automatic coffeemaker and full shower—luxurious in comparison to our humble craft. Boats and floatplanes lay moored in the inlets, sometimes for weeks. When the phalanx of fish arrived, the Department of Fish and Game might let skippers open their nets for twenty minutes. Each migrating school numbered a million or more fish, so a twenty-minute set could mean three hundred tons of herring. The fleet lay in wait for them like a pod of orcas poised for a chase. Only, this pod drank Captain Morgan's spiced rum, played cards, watched videos, and talked about fluctuating fish prices to pass the time.

We moored in a different bay because we were planning to pound herring. We had already hung thousands of kelp leaves into floating cages, or pounds, enclosed with mesh to create underwater corrals. As soon as the herring arrived, we would catch and transfer them into the pounds, hoping they'd spawn onto the kelp, laying up to one thousand eggs on every square inch. We would then box and ship the roe-heavy skeins to sushi restaurants in Japan, which paid top yen for the delicacy.

Jackie had left Kimberly and me on the jitney to wait for the fish, with nothing but a propane stove for heat. It did not really warm up the boat, but it caused condensation to form on the ceiling and walls of the tiny cabin. There was not enough room to stand inside, and even sitting felt cramped, so Kimberly and I huddled under a sleeping bag in the only bunk, drinking Bailey's and coffee. While we were wiping water from the ceiling to stop the dripping, blocks of glacial ice started banging against the hull and the boat shuddered. "If one of these icebergs rips a hole in the boat, we'll drive for shore and just ram this thing onto the beach," I suggested to Kimberly. "It'll ruin the hull, but then again, she left us here to die."

"Why don't you quit putting coffee in with your Bailey's?" Kimberly said. Then she added, "The ice sounds much worse than it really is."

I was a bit wound up from all that caffeine, so I went on deck to smoke a cigarette. Ice chunks surrounded us, bristling against one another. The gray sky's effect of foreboding seemed to lag behind, for snow was already falling—a late-March, unnecessary snow, melting and mixing with salt and returning to the ocean. Squinting, I could make out dark silhouettes lining the beach. When the snowfall lightened, I realized they were hundreds of eagles and seagulls. The gulls' shrieks sounded like war cries as birds swarmed into the sky and began plunging into the ocean. Snow drifted down, the eagles rose, the gulls scattered, and everywhere wings flapped and herring writhed in the vise grip of scaly feet. Gulls swooped for fish the eagles were dropping. Three slick, brown heads surfaced near the pounds, and two more popped up behind the jitney. The sea lions' tails splashed as they dove. A few shook their heads and let out territorial roars, while even more whiskers and noses poked from the water.

Toward shore a tall dorsal fin appeared, pointed like the sheath of a knife, and in an instant, sea lion blood stained the sea vermilion. The dorsal breached into the shiny back of an orca, which—surfacing slowly and diving heavily—swam out of Galena Bay and into Prince William Sound.

Herring carcasses fell from the sky and sea lion blood tinted the ice floes. More eagles arrived. The herring kept coming; the bay bubbled like a cauldron. Fish were spawning along the entire coastline, soothing the bloodied shore with a milky coating, spurning death with millions of eggs, dropping roe from the sky even as eagle talons clutched them.

I thought about calling our skipper and telling her that the herring had arrived, but the jitney's radio did not work. So I just stood on deck in the snow, like a shadow of the industrial world, watching the birds until my feet got cold. Then I went back into the cabin and started another pot of coffee while ice floes jostled the little boat.

A Cure for Despair

CHRISTINE LOWTHER

"What on earth is that noise?"
"More accurate to ask what in the ocean makes it."
"Well, what in the ocean then?"
"That's my resident harbor seal."
"You're kidding?"

This is a conversation I had all summer, whenever visitors came to my floating home in Clayoquot Sound on the west coast of Vancouver Island. A young seal would often rest on one of the flotation logs under my greenhouse and snore. Sometimes it would blow bubbles in the lapping water, which could sound alternately peaceful, humorous, or rude, depending on the seal's whim.

The animal had not yet learned to be shy of humans; this much was evident in its laid-back behavior. Earlier in the season I had heard it crying for its mother over on the rocks beside the island flanking my neighbor's oyster farm. It was a plaintive sound, but I knew not to intervene. This was nature: the mother went fishing and the pup missed her. It was not abandoned. Many times I had heard of people picking up what they thought was an orphaned seal and taking it to some rescue center—causing the permanent separation between parent and offspring that they mistakenly believed had already occurred. On the other hand, I also knew the odd sharp-eyed local who had rescued young seals at death's door.

I frequently got in my kayak and crept close enough to the rocks to spy on the pup through binoculars, making sure it was not at that door. But as long as it continued calling loudly like that, there was a good bet nothing was amiss. It still had strength. It wanted food.

Later, as the seal grew, it seemed to gain some independence and took my little bay for itself. It would surface to inspect whatever humans happened to be paddling around. In general, harbor seals like to follow me, always with a peaceful, slow-breathing presence, patiently watching through those large, liquid eyes. One seal, two, sometimes even three will tag along. They won't come as far as the main channel of Lemmens Inlet, where I venture to look for porpoises; other seals are already there. I am not expert enough to tell them apart. But I did get to know the one that took to swimming near my houseboat. He, or she, was small and lightly colored compared to the other seals, and came closer than them. Much closer.

"No. I'm not kidding. Come see for yourself. You have to tiptoe."

The seal would be hauled-out over a log a mere couple of inches from the floorboards of the greenhouse, between which are wide gaps. Any quiet person could lie down and place an eye to a gap—holding their breath so that the seal wouldn't feel it. I'd look down on the back of its gray head and watch the long whiskers around its nose and study the mottled pattern of its fur. I could hear every nuance of breath, and a sudden snort could be startling.

"Preposterous pinniped!" my wide-eyed marine biologist friend mouthed.

There are, of course, many other animals in my world. I am anchored at a convergence of prime freshwater stream, salt sea, and ancient temperate rainforest. This coming together of habitats teems with wildlife. Black bears wander the shoreline, turning over rocks, munching on small crabs, and grazing on shore grass. Minks emerge from the ocean, shake their gorgeous fur, and scamper up the rocks into the forest. Raccoons dig in the early-morning low-tide mud. The odd snake swims over to my dock to bask in the sun. Bald eagles teach their young to fish. Families of river otters help themselves to my decks, climbing aboard to roll on the warm wood and deposit their droppings. The babies unabashedly run over my solar panels. Otters have growled up at me from between the floorboards. They eat lustily and noisily, crunching on shells and crabs. They are wild. That summer's seal, I liked to tell myself, was not so wild. I pretended it was mine.

It might be closer to the mark to say I was the seal's pet human. I waited for him, looked for him—or her. I thrilled with each sighting and every encounter, marveled over the seal's graceful skill in the water, felt goose bumps and knew I was being watched. I would look up to meet those huge eyes, calmly fixed on me from a position next to one of my land lines, a rope tying one corner of my home to a gnarled tree stump on shore. For a moment, we would both just look.

"Hello, there."

The seal would nonchalantly tip backwards to return to its submarine realm. I often saw it gliding close to the bottom, upside down, ignoring fishes that appeared to tolerate the predator in their midst. At least, they didn't scatter. A spidery, long-legged, slender kelp crab might be creeping along the submerged rope, and when my eyes flicked back from it, the seal would be gone.

Other times, at a distance, a telltale broadcast splash could be heard. It wasn't seals playing, or courting, or arguing. It was seals surrounding schools of fish and scaring hundreds out of the water at once, causing the sound of many small bodies slapping the surface as they fell back down to their doom, or their escape, as the case may be. This feeding technique could be a group effort or carried out by only one seal. Although it must be terrifying for the fish, I always liked the sound—found it soothing, even. I knew that seals, perhaps including my favorite one, were feasting. Splash after splash would fill the bay, sometimes with an echo off the side of Lone Cone Mountain. The sound would travel, but a skilled seal could keep the school in one spot. Less work. More eating.

I never got into the water when the seal was around—at least not in daylight. I had no wish to frighten this creature in its own habitat, its only home, and risk destroying our comfortable, convenient, and to me, deeply satisfying companionship. I had tried swimming with other seals in the past. They had come near enough to ascertain that I was something from which it was better to flee, leaving me disappointed and alone in the cold, briny water. No. I was determined not to scare my young friend. Yet for all I knew it was observing me the few times I did take to the water. I cannot pretend to always have known its whereabouts.

Near the end of September it was time to make the most of the bioluminescence before the autumn storms began, darkening the water and forcing me indoors. Bioluminescence is, quite literally, living light. Dinoflagellates, single-celled, plantlike organisms, produce flashes and submarine sparks through a chemical reaction when agitated. These light effects are pure magic, whether streaming from my paddle with every stroke, or making the faster-swimming fish glow. My friend Maryjka came for a sleepover one night to kayak around the house under the stars—and to create galaxies of her own.

What I did while she paddled about the bay may sound opulent: as on most summer nights, I was enjoying a hot tub. It is funky rather than classy, however. A friend made the tub from salvaged cedar. A solar collector heats it, which means only clear days allow for a nice, hot soak— so hot, in fact, that I take breaks by diving into the ocean, enveloping my body with pale green light.

"Do you think this totem animal of yours will make an appearance?" Maryjka called from the kayak.

"If so, you'll hear breathing close by," I answered from my deeply relaxed state in the tub.

The air was still, trillions of stars dominating the world. The Milky Way was a huge swath of "biolume" curtaining the wide sky that spanned the houseboat.

Soaking away the weariness of peak-tourist-season servitude that bound me to the nearby town of Tofino, I became aware that Maryjka was speaking again. She sounded like she was talking to a baby. I sat up straight and listened more closely.

"Hello sweetie, how *are* you? Oh, so *nice* to see your pretty, *pretty* light show!"

"Uh, Maryjka?"

"Oh, hello, *hello* sweetie!"

"Is it—?"

"It's the seal, look! It's surrounded by bioluminescence! It's a little white cloud that keeps circling the kayak!"

I had never heard her so excited.

"Come in closer," I demanded. She paddled gently up to the float. There. Something like Casper the Ghost, or a seal in photographic negative. A frisky aura scooting around her boat. Then the lights faded. It had surfaced. We could hear it breathing between us. That close.

"I'm getting in."

"*What?*"

"I need to cool off. It won't be afraid of me at night. It'll approach me if I stir up some of my own biolume soup. Whaddya bet? It saw your bright wake and must have come to check you out. This is my last chance to swim with a seal until next year. Why didn't I think of this before?"

As soon as the seal had submerged again, I clambered out of the tub, but instead of diving into the dark sea, I slowly lowered myself in, gripping the deck. The water was heart-stopping, as usual—a great contrast to the temperature of the hot tub. But I was used to going back and forth. I found it invigorating and even a little bit dangerous. And now I was going in with a seal.

Over the years, I have had eyebrows raised at my approach to wild animals. I swim with moon jellyfish. Why not? They don't sting. Once, every swimming guest quickly vacated the ocean onto a deck packed with gawking visitors when a thing like a giant sow bug—with antennae and fourteen legs—zipped by. Me? I jumped in to check it out and got nervous only when it clung to my bathing suit. Another time, I pursued a young cougar, just to make sure I hadn't imagined it. I know there are scores of people who travel vast distances, spend copious cash and undergo various kinds of suffering to get close to wildlife. I'm not all that special. I have read about scientists strongly identifying with their research animals, ignoring extreme weather just to be near them, no longer collecting data. I don't suspect anthropomorphism. I think it is rather akin to love, a fierce longing that makes us reach out from our limited, tame, human selves.

We want to belong to a place in the way they do, to join their ranks like the missing fishermen of legend. We long to shed our skin and don slick fur instead, or at least to have them bestow their blessings.

I did not have to wait long for the seal to come to me. Its streamlined form circled and swished directly beneath me, just out of reach of my stretching toes. Maryjka sat speechless. I gasped with excitement. After a few moments, I felt contact. A quick, careful flipper grazed my heel.

This waterborne creature was not my totem. It was not my pet. Our worlds could only intersect temporarily, with my forays into the ocean and the seal's onto the floats of my houseboat. Nevertheless, I considered it the guardian of my home and sanity. Thinking of it got me through long days of serving tourists, and through worse times as well. Its presence and life joy, its energy and sheer physicality, would protect me from the things that can suck out a soul. When conjured, this sprite would appear without fail: silvery, ethereal, and veiled in brightness.

Once Upon a Whale

LORETTO JONES

Light mist fell on Taku Inlet as I steered *Small Fry* across a glassy sea. Radio talk from other commercial fishermen filled the tiny wheelhouse, and their stories about last night's bad weather broke the stillness of this southeast Alaska fjord. Clouds spilled down green mountainsides in sharp contrast to the night's gale-force winds. I stood on tiptoes and slid open the wheelhouse window, trying to see beyond the fog. There were ten hours left in the salmon opening, and I wanted to be top boat when we sold our catch to the fish buyer.

"*Small Fry, Small Fry.* Got your radio on?" I recognized Bobbi, the other lady skipper, calling my boat.

"Got you here, Bobbi. How's fishing? Geez—did you fish through that storm?"

"Hell no. We tied up in Taku Harbor after gusts blew my radio antenna off the roof."

I grinned at Sean. "We fished until the waves curled over the mast." My young crewmember grimaced, rolling his eyes. "We're pulling out of Troller's Cove now. It's calm—like gliding through mercury. I'm looking for a place to set this net."

Radio static cluttered Bobbi's words. "You're too hungry, always fishing until the end." She laughed, and then became serious. "Hey—heard about that whale?"

"What whale?"

"A humpback whale is trapped in a gill net. The coast guard is monitoring its position off Point Arden. It's drowning. Hey, you're the diver. Give them a call."

I envisioned jumping into the glacier-fed inlet atop a fifty-foot humpback whale tangled in web. Good way to die—snagged then pulled to the depths below. Four currents swept around Point Arden, making it one of the worst areas for tiderips and undertows. No place for a scuba diver.

"Bobbi, your plan doesn't seem so healthy." I had a beautiful two-year-old daughter and more than anything, I wanted to watch her grow up.

"Oh, come on!" Bobbi insisted.

Sean mumbled, "Chick's a psycho," and I nodded in agreement and watched him retreat to the back deck.

"I'm here to make money, Bobbi. Let Greenpeace save the whales." I studied the beach. "Sean," I called out on deck, "let's set. Hey Bobbi, let me call you back. I found a very fishy spot. Gotta go."

"Always about the ka-ching aren't you? I'm going to lose radio contact as soon as I turn the corner. See you . . . " Her voice faded.

Save a whale. How ridiculous was that? Sean popped the orange buoy overboard and I steered, watching him scoop handfuls of cork line, web, and lead line over the stern.

"Can you imagine—a whale letting anyone get close?"

He shook his head.

We leaned against the boat's sides and watched corks bob on the milky surface. The beach disappeared in the fog, but I couldn't stop thinking about the whale. Was it drowning? I closed my eyes, knowing the hopeless terror the whale must feel looking at air inches away, unable to breathe.

It had happened to me three summers ago, off the coast of Baranof Island. I shuddered, recalling how the gray sky receded after my mouthpiece had disconnected from the hose that funneled oxygen to me from the boat. All of a sudden, I had no air. The bag full of abalone dragged me down like an anchor. Water flooded my diving mask. I clawed at the bag's straps but couldn't feel the quick-release through my gloves. I repeatedly fought through thick kelp to the surface only to sink back again. I was two months pregnant and fought for both of us, but I couldn't cut the bag loose or pull off my mask. I passed out. If my dive tender hadn't seen me . . .

I left the back deck and went to the wheelhouse to study the chart. The whale must have been caught in a gill net ditched by a fisherman during the storm. I looked at my watch: nine hours left to fish, eighteen hours since the storm. The whale was running out of time. I flipped the hydraulic winch and called to Sean. "Bring the net aboard."

"What?" he asked. "It's not like you to stop fishing."

"We're heading to Point Arden."

"What? Not the whale?" He looked at me like I'd lost my mind.

"We're going to have a look, okay?"

Fifty minutes later, I saw a small island of green gill net and at its center, wrapped in layers of web, the whale. A white cork had wedged itself into the blowhole. Quickly, I pulled on my drysuit. The whale could hardly breathe.

"Man, that's cruel!" Sean erupted.

A voice boomed over the radio, "Vessel off Point Arden." A quarter mile south, the white hull of a patrol boat was barely visible.

"This is *Small Fry*," I replied.

"*Small Fry, Small Fry*. Be advised. The whale is the property of the United States government."

"Countries don't own whales." I tried to contain my contempt for the mountain of red tape that came from just a radio call. I turned to Sean, "Keep the boat close, but not too close. I'll swim over. We don't want to frighten the whale."

"*Small Fry, Small Fry*." The radioman kept trying.

Sean touched my shoulder, pointing toward a Zodiac streaking across from the coast guard boat. "They're sending the troops over."

The Zodiac swung wide of the whale. The man at the tiller wore a blue wetsuit. He pulled alongside and stopped, holding on to the side of my boat. "My name's Jerry. Permission to come aboard?" He was shorter than me, wearing sunglasses and an infectious smile.

I folded my arms across my chest. "I'm going in to cut that cork out. Now."

"Hey, I'm with you on this. I study whales and want to help. The coast guard provided this skiff." He paused, holding up a form. "This releases the federal government from any liability for—" He laughed. "Just jump in and we'll say you did."

I leaped down into the skiff, clutching two knives. "Let's go."

The whale floated quietly, partly on her side, but when the raft bumped her, she opened her eyes and watched me intently. I leaned over and touched her. Warm skin rippled under my strokes. I grabbed braided cork line and began to cut feverishly until the white cork sailed off on the strong current. Instantly, her exhale of seawater showered us, and Jerry wiped his freckled face with the back of his hand. "Spouted on by a female *Megaptera novaeangliae.*"

"She's female, then?" I asked. He nodded, and under my palm I felt the whale swell, filling her lungs. I watched her blowhole open, then shut, then open. One eye, fluid and wise, scrutinized me when I leaned over again and cut the tough nylon that clung to the bulbous growths on her lower jaw. She was huge. Looking at the crusty collection of barnacles that stippled her chin, I believed her to be ancient. I rested my hand on the supple skin to protect it and felt her body relax. Together, Jerry and I cut away the translucent mesh. It took two hours just to free her long, narrow head.

For years my life had been about taking from the sea and making money. Now none of that seemed important. I caressed the whale, whispering, "I didn't much like drowning either."

Jerry gathered the billowing net I had stripped from the whale. While he pulled it into the Zodiac, I felt her labored breathing slow to a steady rhythm. I wondered if she was a mother like me and had daughters and sons, even grandbabies. "I can't believe I'm touching a whale," I said.

Jerry nodded his head solemnly. "I never knew whales were so soft— and calm. Everyone said the whale would freak out away from her pod."

"My daughter's not going to believe this."

Jerry smiled. "You don't look old enough to be a mom." More net came in over the side. He piled it on the Zodiac's floorboard.

I couldn't get to her other side and so crawled over, lying half in the skiff, half atop the whale. A shudder like an electrical current ran the full length of her body. I was able to reach down and clear web stuck to the pectoral fins just below her shoulder blade. I pulled myself over and sat fully astride the whale. I must have looked silly yanking at the net, but it would not come loose. "The lead line is wrapped around her fluke."

Jerry stood staring at me. "Aren't you afraid she's going to sound?"

"I haven't thought about it." And that was the truth. Who was the psycho now? I slid off her back into the Zodiac, joining Jerry on the web pile draped over the boat's side.

The whale was five times longer than the raft and continued to drift quietly alongside.

I tried to peer through the fog, looking for *Small Fry*, worried about Sean. The coast guard boat too, had disappeared. "Have you got a handheld VHF?"

Jerry pitched the plastic bag with the radio and I opened it, pushing the call button.

"*Small Fry, Small Fry*, can you read me?"

"How's the whale?" Sean's voice crackled from the radio.

"Breathing. Listen—soon the tide will start flooding into the inlet. Stay close. This fog is getting thicker."

"She's going to make it?"

"I hope so."

"Good. I'll stay close. Hey, good luck."

Without warning the Zodiac tipped, pulled down as the whale began to submerge. I watched in horror as the rubber skiff took on water. The net started to float, snagging everything—gas can, anchor, and oars. We'd never get free if she dove. Together, we hastily shoved the net overboard. Cold seawater continued to pour over the side and we started to roll over. I snatched a handful of web and started hacking while Jerry cleared a snarl from the oarlock. Desperate, I called to her, slapping the water several times with my hand as I'd seen whales do with their tails, hoping she'd surface. Within moments she rose, and I could see she was struggling to stay afloat under the lead and net's relentless grip. We scrambled to dislodge the oarlock and watched the net avalanche after the whale. The

Zodiac flopped back, full of water. I started to bail.

"That was too close." Jerry almost choked on his words.

I slumped against the raft's tube, shaking. Jerry's teeth did a jig. Hypothermia was taking its toll after exposure to cold water for more than eight hours.

"Where'd she go?" Jerry asked, waiting for the whale to show again. Suddenly, off toward the beach, five hundred feet from the raft, she resurfaced and rested—waiting for us to catch up?

"We have to free her flippers," I said.

"What do you think about cutting the remainder of the net from her tail?" Jerry asked.

"It would be suicide. One accidental flip and we'd be history, but she needs her flippers to navigate." The Zodiac once again nudged up to the whale. "I'm going in."

"But you said—," Jerry hesitated.

"I'm not going near the tail." I put on my mask and slipped over the side, careful to avoid the web's trap. I had decided to leave the scuba tank, fearing the valve would tangle or worse yet, the bubbles would frighten her. Inhaling deeply, I free-dove, holding my breath while swimming around the head, her right eye watching closely. Eye to eye, I pleaded without words. *Don't move, please.* She could sound anytime, taking me with her. I concentrated on the nylon that shackled her flippers, careful not to become ensnared. In many places strands had sawed into the skin, leaving bloody gashes. I came up gasping for breath. I swam around and held on to her other flipper, a scallop-edged wing, thick and powerful and more than five feet long. It felt slick as rubber. I clung in awe to the whale, realizing that with one stroke—I could die. Pulling myself down along the whale's side I cut my hand on the barnacles that colonized both ridges of her chin. I watched my blood ribbon into saltwater and then began the delicate process of removing the web, working until I was out of air. On the third dive I arced underwater and slid the dull side of my blade against the whale's flesh while the edge cut the net until her flipper was free.

The whale didn't move until I had crept back into the boat, completely spent. Gently, she pushed away from the Zodiac, her flippers spread wide.

She could maneuver now and in an instant was flying through the sea. We followed her toward Greely Point, where a red marker warned of a ragged reef that juts into the inlet.

"Why is she running from us?" Jerry asked, concerned.

"She's not running. She's headed for the reef to strip the remaining line and web off her tail." We watched as she dove, the lead line trailing from her broad fluke.

A west wind from across the bay dispersed the fog. As sky holes opened, rays of sunlight permeated the world. *Small Fry* wallowed fifty feet from us. Jerry's teeth were chattering between plum-colored lips. He jumped up and down, trying to warm up. "I'm freezing."

"Me too." My whole body trembled. "Take me back to my b-b-boat."

Jerry laughed and turned the Zodiac toward *Small Fry*, where Sean waited on deck. Sunlight burned through the fog and up high, cirrus wisps flecked a cobalt sky. The patrol boat appeared out of a melting fog bank, headed straight toward us. Jerry steered cautiously alongside *Small Fry* while Sean reached down for our line.

"We did it," I said.

"That we did," Jerry said. His ice-blue eyes twinkled.

"You still want me to sign that release?"

"Nah," he grinned. "It got lost . . . somehow."

"I better get this fish to market before my tender leaves the area." We waved as Jerry wheeled the Zodiac toward the patrol boat. Sean unzipped my drysuit and I hurried below to the warm stove.

"Made a fresh pot of coffee," Sean said. "Can you believe it? You saved a whale."

"*We* saved a whale, Sean. All of us." I touched the color photo of my two-year-old taped above the compass. "Wait till I tell you this bedtime story."

"Steer us home, Sean," I said, tugging the drysuit's tight neck seal over my head and peeling it down around my shoulders. I huddled by the oil stove, drying my long hair. I could not believe I'd been on a whale.

The boat's engine powered down unexpectedly. Sean shouted, "Quick! You got to see this." I stumbled upstairs to the wheelhouse. In front of *Small Fry* the whale breached, rising straight out of the waves into the air, before gracefully falling back into the sea and flipping her tail as if in farewell. Fresh rips oozed blood, but no net remained. We heard a whoop from the radio, and I recognized Jerry's excited voice along with the rest of the patrol-boat crew, which traveled behind us.

I ran out on deck and watched her roll in the waves, seawater glistening against her flanks. "You are beautiful!" I shouted. With each muscular tail thrust she gained speed, and then she pivoted, splashing playfully. Before long she approached *Small Fry*. She stopped about ten feet away, as if waiting. I wanted to jump back in and share her newfound freedom. In a final gesture she waved her flipper, bringing it down hard on the green sea. We did not speak the same language. But I understood.

She lingered another moment and then slipped back under, headed for open water.

Eye of the Storm

JAMES MICHAEL DORSEY

On the glacier-bound waters of Alaska's Inside Passage, sound skips like a flat stone, distorting distance and betraying those who would move silently through the morning fog.

The blowing of several orcas punctures the mist, and I sense they are near.

It is summer, and transient whales are following schools of salmon heading north to spawn. Skimming the sea without sound, a kayak is the perfect vehicle to their domain.

A year ago, while paddling near this very spot, I witnessed the whales conducting a funeral. The sky set the mood for this somber event, dull gray and drizzly, as Alaska summers can be.

I was pushing my kayak through kelp forests when I heard the first blow. A large bull led the way, cruising the mist like an apparition. He was bearing a stillborn calf across his rostrum. The calf, still flushed pink, slumped across his snout, limp as a rag doll, its head and flukes underwater. The bull traveled deliberately, neither blowing nor porpoising, and five smaller whales trailed it single file into deep water at the channel's center. There the bull stopped, holding his lifeless charge while the other whales surrounded him. He then lowered his head, letting the dead whale slip into the depths.

The pain of loss hung in the air, thicker than fog.

An old female, most likely the matriarch, lob-tailed the water twice, perhaps in farewell, or else just a signal that they were finished. But as she did this, all six orcas came abreast and dove in unison. They knew I was there and ignored me.

This memory floods over me as I hear the familiar blows. I stop paddling and scan the fogbank. They are close.

It is cold this morning, and calm. The sun has tried to break through twice without success. The silence is pierced only by the cry of a lone eagle clawing fish from the littoral. Minnows are jumping, a sure sign that larger fish are about. I can see my breath and therefore zip up my fleece.

A young sea lion pops up, lunges for my boat, and startles me into action. He clearly is terrified, seeking refuge ahead of my bow.

In a different situation I might let him rest, but I fear what is coming, and he cannot stay. I slap the water hard with my paddle. He veers, if only for a second; this animal is truly scared. He approaches a second time, and I fend him off with the flat of my blade, looking into innocent eyes as he arches for a dive. He disappears, leaving behind a trail of bubbles.

Silver flashes under my boat, and a second later I am hit square in my chest by a salmon. It flops onto the spray skirt, flailing to get back into the water. Then one fish after another strikes the side of my boat.

Suddenly a dorsal fin cuts the fog like an obsidian blade bearing down on me, causing a white wake.

The first orca crosses my bow, snapping up a fish in midair. Before I can react, a dozen hungry hunters surround me.

The pod is herding salmon, driving them against a rock wall twenty yards to my port. Whales form a semicircle around my boat, and they have the salmon cornered. The fish run in panic while shiny fins slice the water, churning it crimson red as they round up their prey. Salmon slam headfirst into the rock wall, getting knocked senseless. I am in the eye of a cetacean storm.

These carnivores have gathered around my boat on numerous occasions and always been curious and friendly. To the best of my knowledge they have never attacked a person or boat. They are ruthless hunters, yet gentle when contacting people. Still, I fight an upwelling of panic and sit in awe as a deadly ballet plays out around me.

A white saddle patch zips underneath the boat, rolling at the last second to miss my keel, while another whale swims parallel to it, showering me with exhale as it swoops in for a kill. Glistening dorsals cross left and right of me; bodies part the water like torpedoes. I can feel their echoing clicks and squeals through the fiberglass hull of my boat. Despite my presence, they are executing a perfectly choreographed hunt.

Salmon leap in all directions, clearing the water with muscular grace. Bulky heads breach the water, raking fish from midair. One whale streaks toward my broadside, and I instinctively brace for the collision. At the very last moment he swings wide, taking a life as he dives.

The whales course within inches of my boat, some even grazing it—but they know I am here and avoid confrontation. I sit stock-still, not wishing to press my luck.

I am soaked from their spouting and covered with the bloody confetti of fish scales. Twice I must brace against the thrashing and carefully push a hunk of salmon flesh off my deck with my paddle, not wishing to tempt a hungry whale.

For most of an hour the orcas fish, then, gradually, the action slows. They have eaten their fill, and I see Dall's porpoises snagging a few stragglers. Orcas often allow their smaller cousins to join a hunt, usually near the end to clean up leftovers.

The final act is something I have never before seen.

Half the pod forms a single line, parallel to the cliff, turning their flukes toward it. They begin to lob-tail, and the resulting waves break against rocks. They are dislodging the few salmon that hide in the crevices and cracks, while the rest of the gang and the porpoises scoop up what is left. Before long, the whales switch from feeding frenzy to lethargy, lolling around my boat like gigantic stuffed sausages.

The sudden calm allows me to survey them at leisure, and I realize they are all females or juvenile males—not one mature bull amongst them. While orcas form matriarchal societies, an alpha bull normally stands guard. This hunt was sanctioned on his watch. I know he is somewhere nearby.

I try to imagine where I would place myself as the protector of a dozen feeding whales and paddle farther into the channel to sit and wait him out.

Within a minute the tip of his tall dorsal rises; the wind carries a soft blow toward me, mixed in with the fog's droplets. I am sitting by the great whale, no more than thirty feet away.

He came up as smooth and stealthy as a submarine; now his fin towers five feet above me. Sunlight sparks on his ebony back, and his saddle patch gleams like a snowfield. His dorsal is slightly bent; a missing chunk tells me he has met at least one large shark. He is half again as long as my boat and outweighs me by nine tons. He is a flesh eater whose teeth can shred a great white. I am sitting alone next to the greatest predator ever to rule the ocean. He logs on the surface fully at ease, sure of his power, in control of his realm. I am insignificant, an interloper, here by his indulgence.

He has not appeared by chance, as he is too smart. He chose the place and time to show himself and is making a statement.

I am still alive not by accident. My boat floats between him and his kin—a position he would never grant to an enemy. If he thought me a threat to the pod, I would be dead like the salmon. He knew of my presence possibly long before the hunt began and not only tolerated me but allowed me to witness. I understand this as if he were talking to me.

Perhaps I have been designated a mere curiosity, but I choose to think of this as communication. His dark eye, no larger than the tip of my thumb, fixates me as I try to fathom the intelligence behind it.

Fearing to overstay my welcome, I dip my paddle in slow motion and pull away. As I do, the bull as well inches ahead at minimum speed. I paddle a bit harder and he stays with me, so I dig in and shovel water behind me, my bow cutting a wake. The bull starts to pass me, then senses frailty and checks his speed to match mine, even and steady.

His head undulates, eye just below the waterline, watching, urging me on. He asks me to paddle with him and I accept the challenge.

Even in his lowest gear it is hard for me to keep up. But I am now part of his pod—he is the leader—and this will never happen again. I crank up my paddle strokes, abandoning all technique, trying to maintain speed. My arms scream with pain, but time flows like molasses. All that matters now is that I stay with this great beast.

For a brief interval there is only the two of us moving as one, and if ever an animal gave a gift to man, this is mine.

I have no idea how far we have come, but soon I can go no farther. I rest my paddle across the cockpit and glide to a halt. I am cold, wet, exhausted, and have never been more alive.

The great whale sees I have stopped and lingers an instant before diving. For a few seconds I am completely alone, and the silence is deafening. I look all around and feel very small. He resurfaces in the distance where the pod is assembling. The bull may be reporting to the matriarch, telling of the strange creature that entered their space.

Before long, they turn their flukes toward me and swim off. The fog closes in again, and I watch fins fade into it as if this were some kind of an ending. I sit, sucking air, trying to grasp what just happened.

An eagle cries far away. I turn my bow toward land to paddle home.

Watching

NANCY LORD

The sound got my attention first.

I was walking back along the beach, just after low tide, after having checked the sets where my partner, Ken, and I place our gill nets on fishing days. I'd tightened fixed lines and retrieved an extender line left tied to a buoy—standard tasks on the off days between fishing periods. I was, as usual, lost in thought, an occupational advantage of the kind of commercial salmon fishing I'd done for fifteen summers on the remote western shore of Alaska's Cook Inlet. For me, a favorite part of fishing—after hauling in nets full of shining fish, enough to fill the skiff bottom and stack toward the gunnels—is the quiet, meditative time spent walking the beach or rocking, waiting, in the open skiff.

If my mind had taken a Zen turn, that didn't mean I was oblivious to the world around me. That day I was carefully keyed to a few particular and essential points of awareness: the placement of my feet on rocks, the state of the tide (which rushes in and out of Cook Inlet in one of the world's greatest tidal exchanges), and any movement along the beach (which frequently turns out to be a bear absorbed in tasks of its own).

The sound of breathing brought my head up and turned me to the water. The exhalations were both familiar and distinctive: "poofing" percussions, blows with both liquid and airy dimensions. They're never much to see. Certainly not spouts, they're at most short mists. On this calm day, with the inlet as smooth as polished pewter, the whales' risings cut the surface like knife blades, and the whales' breaths were remarkable only—and sufficiently—by being audible. For as far as I could see, a long stream of belugas was proceeding north with the tide, looking like a sudden swatch of whitewater along the shore. I stood just in from the water's edge in gray mud among rounded cobbles, and they passed just beyond that border, through the element that was muddy gray water, across the same cobbled bottom. The closest ones weren't thirty feet offshore, and they couldn't have been in much more water than would cover them. They must have been nearly brushing bottom as they passed, dodging the boulders that lay in their paths.

My eyes swept the line of them, dozens at a time showing some slice of brilliant white skin. Up and under and up again. The belugas, trooplike, were rolling forward at a steady, traveling pace. In any snapshot of time I was catching sight of only a fraction—a fourth? a fifth?—of them; the whole pod had to number well over one hundred. I fixed my eyes on a particular whale and watched it arch through the water, its smooth back gleaming. It looked like nothing so much as a wheel, a round white disk churning the sea. It turned under and then, a few beats later, rose up again fifty yards ahead. The turn of another glistening wheel, and then I looked ahead, and there it rose again, and then it was too far from me, and I chose another closer whale to follow. Then I looked across them all and marveled at the sea of them: white wheels turning. Some were larger, some were whiter, some were paired—swimming close and rising together. Some were young and smaller and gray, more difficult to see in the mud-colored water, above and beside and slightly behind the larger belugas that were their mothers. Like geese in a V formation or bicyclists in a pack, those young were getting a ride, a hydrodynamic assist.

I looked more closely at individual rising whales, trying to catch them at the first break in the water's surface, trying to snatch a view of something other than that quick white arch. In other places where belugas live, and perhaps in other parts of the inlet when they're doing something other than traveling, these whales will lift their heads from the water as though looking around. They hang vertically in the water and bob upward—

"spy-hopping," biologists and whale watchers call it. They slap flippers and tails, float at the surface, and otherwise show themselves in more of their dimensions. But here, at this point of land between broad bays, the whales always seemed to pass back and forth without lingering and with frustratingly little show. Here, where the currents run fast, I'd at best seen an occasional fluke flip up into the air.

This time, I was close and the light was good, and when I was quick to set my eyes on a whale just beginning to surface, I could glimpse the bulbous swelling that was the back of the head before the narrowing that makes a neck, and then—especially if the whale was turned slightly toward shore—the knobbiness of the vertebrae along its back. And again, I was looking at a wheel turning, those knobs like gear teeth.

I had, of course, seen photographs of belugas, and I knew they were nothing like that illusion of round, turning wheel. An entire beluga looks, in fact, something like the lumpy Pillsbury Doughboy. Belugas are not full bodied like other whales, and they're certainly not streamlined, not sleek, not as beautiful as we imagine creatures that slide through the sea to be. I knew as I watched the whales pass along the beach that the ten- to sixteen-foot bodies I couldn't see were shaped more like poorly rolled cigars, bulging and gaunt in odd places, with small, bulbous heads and pathetically blunted, petal-shaped flippers. As whales go, belugas are not fast swimmers—one reason that, where there are killer whales (as there sometimes are in Cook Inlet), they travel this close to shore; they can't outswim their predators but they *can* swim in very shallow water. I knew, too, that those bulbous heads, if I could only see them, were famous for their expressiveness. Belugas have mouths that smile.

Only once had I seen a beluga body in full—a dead one washed up on our beach the summer before. It was swollen and smelly, its skyward eye plucked out by birds, its mouth open to peg teeth, its skin sunburned pink and brown. It was not a lovely creature. Still, I looked hard at it there on the beach, filling my sight with the bulk of it so that when I saw, again, the mere crescent of a back, I might at least complete the idea of the whole to which it belonged. Ken and I briefly wondered what had caused the death;

we saw nothing obvious and were not concerned. Death was, we knew, natural enough. Bears came and ate the dead beluga, and then there were only greasy bones.

Later, however, we wondered a little more. Ken studied the teeth in the jaw and pulled one out when it loosened from its flesh. The teeth were many and fierce—not the worn-down stubs of an elderly animal that had reached the end of a long life. Some disease maybe? Something it had eaten that it shouldn't have? Had it stranded and died on another beach before washing onto ours? Had it been caught in a fishing net and drowned? Had it been shot?

We knew that in the old days, fishermen sometimes shot at belugas—either because they didn't like them eating fish or because shooting was fun. But that had stopped twenty years before with the passage of the federal Marine Mammal Protection Act in 1972. The penalties for taking or harassing whales and other marine mammals were severe, and aside from that, those old attitudes about whales being nuisance predators were, well, *old*.

One exception to marine mammal protection provided for subsistence hunting by Alaska Natives, that is, traditional hunting rights were also protected, and Alaska's Indians, Eskimos, and Aleuts could take from most marine mammal populations what they needed for food and crafts. Villagers throughout Alaska lived with the seasonal sequences of fishing, berrying, and hunting—providing their families with the foods they depended on for both nutrition and cultural value. Cook Inlet, the long estuary reaching up through southcentral Alaska—from the Gulf of Alaska to the city of Anchorage between two arms at its head—is home to most of Alaska's human population and much of its industry. Certainly belugas had been a source of food for the region's early people, but times had changed. Natives I knew—both along my fishing beach in the upper inlet and from villages near my winter home in Homer, in the lower inlet—hunted seals and otherwise depended to a great degree on the bounty of the sea, but they did not go after belugas. I thought the village of Tyonek, to our north, might still take an occasional one.

It was an extraordinary thing, when I stopped to think about it: that we should have whales in such a place, at such a point in time.

In 1992 nearly four hundred thousand people lived both around Cook Inlet and up its streams and rivers. Elsewhere in the world where you found people in such numbers, whales and other large (and small) creatures generally had a hard time of it, and they generally didn't last. Why should Cook Inlet be different? For more than a century, commercial fishermen had been removing salmon and other fish from its waters. People cleared land and eroded riverbanks. Ships and barges traveled through the waters. From my spot on the beach, I looked across the inlet's narrowest part; on the far shore, a vaporous white plume rose and merged into the billows of cumulous clouds building over farther mountains. The plume, from an ammonia plant, was cleaner now than it used to be when the spruce trees all around the plant were killed by its gases. Beside the plant, rows of huge tanks gleamed whitely, and a tanker, loading liquefied gas, rested at the dock. To the north, oil platforms flared their orange flames. The inlet was a busy place, surrounded by and filled with competing uses, and under enormous developmental pressures.

In Anchorage, office workers spotted belugas from their desks. In Kenai, just down the road from the ammonia plant and the tank farm, friends who lived by the river heard the breaths of belugas through their open windows. Down in Homer, families made a Mother's Day tradition out of driving out the Homer Spit to watch lines of belugas swim past the hotel. We had all that contact, and still nobody seemed to know very much about Cook Inlet's beluga whales.

I probably knew as much about belugas as any ordinary citizen. I knew they were called sea canaries for the variety of sounds—clicks, whistles, chatterings, chirps, trills, buzzes, grunts, and pops—they made by blowing and vibrating air through passages around their larynges and blowholes. Some sounds are associated with communication among themselves. Other sounds, principally the clicks, are used in echolocation—that is, the whales bounce the sounds they make off objects and then receive and process the echoes in the oil-filled structures of their heads to "see" what's in their environment. Mariners in wooden ships used to hear beluga songs resonating in the hulls, and some said that blowhole whistling carried clearly through the air. The fact that I'd never heard so much as a squeak was a disappointment to me—and something I attributed to the nature of beluga traveling behavior, which seemed a straight-ahead and silent business.

I knew as well that belugas had as their own close relatives the single-horned narwhals, which were as fantastic as unicorns, and that they were (generally speaking) Arctic whales—hence the lack of a dorsal fin, which could be a problem in ice, and the substitution of a hardened dorsal ridge. I'd seen the range of beluga coloration and knew the animals started out gray, gradually whitening into maturity. And I knew they had "necks"— unfused vertebrae that allowed them to turn their heads.

My local museum had on display an articulated beluga skeleton, and the bones were a giveaway to the whale's evolutionary past as a land mammal: inside the flipper the skeletal design looked very much like a hand, and back where a pelvis may once have been floated two small, unattached bones reduced to connecting muscles. The museum also owned a couple of rocks taken from a beluga stomach—suggesting that belugas did, at least sometimes, feed on the inlet's floor.

I'd been intrigued with the various names we humans have given belugas—names that remark one way or another on appearance. The scientific name, *Delphinapterus leucas*, had not been affixed until the late date of 1776; it means "white dolphin without a wing" (*wing* meaning, in this case, a dorsal fin). The common name "beluga"—or as some prefer, "belukha"—comes from Russian. I knew from studying Russian that *byeli* meant white and that names deriving from colors often have the ending *kha*—thus, "white one." (The belukha spelling and pronunciation eliminates confusion with the completely unrelated beluga sturgeon, from which come the fish eggs valued as caviar.) The English called the beluga the white whale, a name often still used (and not to be confused with the white whale of *Moby-Dick*, which was an albino sperm whale). Most recently, I'd learned that in the Dena'ina Athabaskan language of Cook Inlet the name for beluga was either *qunshi* or *quyushi*, which translates as "that which comes up."

Belugas in the world are not particularly rare. Relatively large numbers (perhaps sixty thousand) seasonally inhabit the waters of western Alaska. More than one hundred thousand form the worldwide circumpolar population. In the scientific arena, there is little urgency to study them, and work in Arctic waters has never been easy. Cook Inlet is one of a very few southerly regions where belugas are found, but our whales have never been given much attention. No one knows how many there are. No one knows where they go in winter when they seem to disappear. Scientists only speculate they are a stock separate from any other belugas—that they stay in Cook Inlet or in the Gulf of Alaska and do not intermix with any other belugas.

I liked that I lived with mystery whales.

The stream of whales reached its tail end, and I stepped back from the water's edge to watch the stragglers from atop a sun-warmed rock. Had they even known I was there?

Sometimes when Ken and I were on the beach together, we'd call to one another to look at the whales, and even with us running back and forth and being boisterous, the whales seemed to pay no attention to us. Sometimes when we were fishing from the skiff, we'd look up to find whales passing nearby, again seemingly undisturbed by our presence or by the sound of our outboard, and always avoiding our nets. These were times when we liked nothing better than to kill our motor and drift among the whales. It was as close as we ever got to their watery world, to being tossed by the same waves they were tossed by, and we felt, cradled there within our curved metal skin, almost like their reverse images—creatures of the dry side as they were of the wet.

But there were other times, when the whales passed the beach at low tide, that I would try to get close by rock-hopping out onto the reef in front of our camp, only to have the whales spook. One moment they were there, and then they were gone, headed wide or simply down and on, out of sight. I suspected the passing whales this day were aware of my standing, then sitting, at the water's edge and that they had not found me particularly threatening.

And then they were all by the point and around into Trading Bay, and I was left staring at the gray inlet that was flat and still except for the currents that swept past, rumbling around the giant, rounded rocks exposed by the tide.

Salmon—red salmon, sockeyes—were moving with the tide, too, invisible in the murk unless one should throw itself clear in an acrobatic leap or, in water so smooth, crease the surface with its dorsal fin. They were, in any case, safe from our nets until the next fishing period two days off. Other unseen creatures shared the waters—starry flounder skimming the bottom, Dolly Varden trout, colorful red and green Christmas anemones flailing from the sides of rocks, a saucer-eyed seal that might at any moment bob its head clear. Upper Cook Inlet, with its load of sediment, is not the world's richest marine environment, but millions of salmon headed for their nascent streams and lakes pass through every summer. I was there because of salmon, and so were the belugas, the seals, the trout that follow the salmon to feed on their eggs and fry, the bottom fish, and the invertebrates that partake of what comes down to them.

Water was visibly flooding in over the flats, moving up the beach, surrounding the rock on which I perched. An eagle squawked. The breeze, warmed to tepid by its passage over sun-soaked mud and sand, brushed my bare arms and stirred the alders on the hillside. I ached as I do when the gifts of the place would catch me unaware. The West Foreland and Cook Inlet are, in general, hard places, and a person has to be tough to live there, whether on the beach or water. I kill fish for a living. I am not generally given to sentiment, don't gush over animals, and have no desire to pat whales on their heads. But I *did* like beluga whales, and I *did* appreciate living in a time and place that sustained fish, whales, and fishermen—all of us together.

It wasn't every day that belugas passed my door. But it was often enough throughout the summer months to remind me just how fortunate I was.

After all, I might have remained in New Hampshire. Growing up there, I'd never seen a whale—or an eagle, for that matter—and my concept of "beach" had been Hampton, part of the tiny and excessively crowded New Hampshire coastline, where on hot summer days it was nearly impossible to find a towel-size square to call one's own.

Our first week in Alaska, Ken and I, paddling a kayak across Kachemak Bay in a late-night, dusky calm, found ourselves surrounded by circling black fins. In our ignorance, I'd thought them sharks, and Ken imagined killer whales. That our companions were only porpoises made the experience scarcely less memorable; here we would live with whales and other finned and flippered creatures.

And we did: killer whales alongside a salmon tender we ran in Prince William Sound, humpbacks leaping into the light beyond a window where I wrote one winter in Sitka, gray whales slapping their enormous chins while a friend and I cut salmon at the end of the Alaska Peninsula. Minke whales sped around our bay, and once, walking behind our house in Homer, Ken and I spotted some much-larger whale's tall blow, a mile off, fall back to sea. A dead fin whale washed up, and we hiked with friends to the lovely beach to look upon its length.

I learned along the way to divide whales into their two groupings of toothed and baleen, that the nearly exterminated right whales were called that because they were the "right" whales for whalers to go after (that is, they were loaded with oil and floated when dead), and that at least some biologists preferred to call killer whales "killer whales" instead of "orcas" because they wanted to acknowledge their predatory nature and not pretend that all whales were peaceable-kingdom pacifists. Our living room windowsill at home began to collect—among agates and glass fishing floats—odd chunks and strips of beach-combed baleen. At museums, I looked with sharpened interest at Native-made baleen baskets and at lonely sailor scrimshawing on sperm whale teeth. I read *Moby-Dick* for a first and second time.

But it was belugas, small and relatively undramatic, that we lived with, summer after summer. When we crossed the inlet by plane, we were accustomed to seeing pods of them below us, looking like expanses of whitecaps in the middle of wide water. At camp, our skiff drifted among them, and I tried to cup my ear to the deck to listen for their singing. When we got together with our neighbors on the beach, we talked about them: "Did you see . . . " and "There were a lot of young ones," and "Yeah, there was a pilot whale with them."

My rock had become an island, the eagle had sailed off, and the whales were long gone. Other chores beckoned from my cabin, up the beach, beside the creek, where our yellow Don't Tread on Me flag hung limply from its pole. I headed home.

Little did I know, that July day in 1992, that the whales I'd stopped to watch—that I'd unquestioningly assumed to be a constant in my life—were in trouble. In the summers to follow, fewer whales passed my beach and they passed on fewer occasions. Within a few years, I watched all season without seeing a single beluga.

Summer after summer after summer, I kept watch for belugas. On calm days at my camp, I tracked, without thinking, the tide changes, and I found myself looking toward the point the whales would round—if only they would—on the flood. On rougher days, my eyes caught on the tops of waves, tricking me into white illusions. On the quietest nights, when the water barely brushed the shoreline, I lay in bed, and in half consciousness I heard that rhythmic wash as the exhalations of whales. I lifted my face to the window and looked out over the beach and the empty gray water, and then I lay down again and listened to the breathing in my dreams.

POSTSCRIPT

(Postscript: endurance; preservation; propagation; sustenance; swan song; tenacity.   —Roget's Thesaurus)

The Last of Its Kind

MICHAEL ENGELHARD

E yes watering in a breeze that snatched its sting from the pack ice, I scan the coastal plain for signs of life. My binoculars frame horizon segments blurred by the midsummer sun, a mindbender like Prudhoe Bay's gas flares, which gyrate above industrial installations one hundred and fifty miles to the west. A liquid glare melds earth and sky. Distant "lakes" separate then coalesce, dissolving terra firma into quicksilver, a landscape of uncertainties. When polar fronts straddle warm ground, light flexes into mirages like this, supple and transient as tundra denizens. More than other places perhaps, and not without irony, the continent's northern fringe suggests limits; its luminous emptiness unmoors assumptions, urging us to reconsider the scale of things, their importance, and beyond that, the scope of our ambitions.

I focus on a boulder pair adrift amongst tussocks on this inland sea. Changing position ever so slightly, the mounds look too bulky to be grizzlies as well as the wrong shade of brown. Propelled by a "Forward, hard!" our blue rubber raft scrapes across gravel, its blunt snout nuzzling shore. Ravines and willow clusters downwind from two grazing musk oxen allow us to sneak up on them single file and hunched over in an effort to reduce our silhouettes, to appear small and nonthreatening. Screened by topography as much as by the animals' poor eyesight, we pause frequently, considering how far we should push our luck. The jingling of digital cameras alone could invite an attack. We also don't want to harass the roaming haystacks; it is *their* refuge after all, though we need it just as badly.

One hundred yards. Fifty. The bulls raise their prizefighter heads, sampling the wind. The dark masses seem to draw sunlight, to collect gravity like black holes on the hoof. We freeze. Catching sight of us, they neither charge nor turn tails but high-step away, nimble as dancers despite their weight, the hemlines on their wool skirts trim and swaying in sync with dainty, white-stockinged feet.

When musk oxen feel threatened they circle or line up in front of their calves like armored cars on a parade ground, a reaction honed through millennia of skirmishes with bears and wolves. An alpha bull may break rank without advance notice. Taut as a spring, he will launch from a wall of fur, horns, and bossed foreheads, ready to gore or throw any intruder. (Incredibly, one rutting bull lunged at a low-flying airplane in an attempt to hook the landing gear.) While a circling-the-wagons instinct served musk oxen well before the advent of humans, it contributed to their decline throughout Alaska before the mid-1800s. For centuries Inuit hunters had used dogs in pursuit of fleeing herds, forcing *oominqmak*—the Bearded Ones—to align within range of arrows or spears. Yankee whalers wintering in the western Canadian Arctic and traders who provisioned them with meat or skins used rifles instead, felling animals one at a time long distance. Whole kin groups faced death bisonlike, with the composure of statues. Expeditions wanting live specimens for zoos had to annihilate parental bulwarks before they could capture the calves sheltered behind them.

Tied closer to sparse rangelands, with large bodies harder to sustain, musk oxen have always been less numerous than caribou. During the Pleistocene, herds flowed back and forth across much of the ice-free interior, western, and all of northern Alaska, contemporary with mammoths and mastodons; but climate changes during the Holocene probably hastened the erstwhile demise of a species sculpted by glaciers and wind.

Trying to restore the region's biodiversity, the federal government imported thirty-four musk oxen from Greenland in 1930. By ship and by train, the transplants arrived in Fairbanks. Five years later, thirty-one animals were crated and then barged to Nunivak Island in the Bering Sea, where they prospered. In 1969 and 1970, Nunivak musk oxen were shipped to northern Alaska, including sixty-three animals that laid the foundation for a herd in the Arctic National Wildlife Refuge, the state's contested northeastern corner. Upon their release, several confused musk oxen wandered onto the sea ice, but Eskimo herders on snowmachines pushed them back to shore. The new herd grew and dispersed for the next fifteen years, expanding their range as far west as Prudhoe Bay. In 1986 the refuge population peaked, numbering close to four hundred animals.

To everybody's surprise, a 2006 survey of traditional musk ox habitat north of the Continental Divide came up short. Although musk oxen can be difficult to spot from the air and some may have been overlooked, their numbers were down everywhere, and pilots counted only a single animal within the refuge boundaries. It is easy to imagine that loner as one of the two shag piles our boat crew approached on the Aichilik River, which unbeknownst to us then could have been the entire herd.

A layer of guard hairs on top of luxurious underwool known as *qiviut* will keep musk oxen cozy at forty below. Qiviut's density and insulation value—seven times that of sheep wool—are directly related to the animal's defense tactics; if, like caribou, musk oxen were to bolt from their enemies instead of bunching up, they would quickly overheat. Though not quite as precious as gold, qiviut is as coveted: two ounces of the gossamer yarn—a ball the size of a small grapefruit—sell for a hundred dollars or more. With a yield of up to four pounds per hide, pressure from subsistence hunters could easily have played a role in the decline, at least until 2006, when musk ox hunting in the Arctic National Wildlife Refuge was suspended.

Biologists believed that, regardless of its legendary fleece, the refuge's last musk ox would not survive another winter.

What triggered this downward slide of a species that has weathered far-flung glaciation? Poaching? A mysterious disease? Toxins in the water or soil?

Residents of Kaktovik, an Inupiaq village nestled against the Arctic Ocean's blue sweep, increasingly comment on erratic weather, which may afflict musk oxen. Colder springs delay breakup season, preserving snowdrifts deep enough to stop even nine-hundred-pound bulls. Untimely thaw-freeze episodes encase grasses and sedges under an ice crust too thick to be cracked by hooves. Malnourished cows may give birth to weak calves, or leave in search of greener pastures in the Brooks Range or Canada. Not too long ago, thirteen musk oxen drowned in a flood on the Colville River west of the refuge; others got stranded on raw barrier islands where they pawed sand for sustenance and starved to death after the sea ice melted, mingling their bones with bleached driftwood.

Perhaps more disturbing to people who view wilderness as simply another theme park or Garden of Eden, some North Slope grizzlies figured out how to breach musk ox formations. Since 1998, refuge biologists have found evidence of bears killing between two and six musk oxen from different groups, sometimes without utilizing all the meat. Gradually, grizzlies perfected their hunting technique: avoiding curved-dagger horns, they bite behind shoulder humps where life runs close to the surface, severing their prey's spinal cord. Not all bears became experts, however; a few have been wounded—at least one even mortally—battling the North's largest land mammals.

Although they are rare, multiple or "surplus" killings have been recorded for species ranging from spiders to orcas. Most cases occur when risk-and-effort scales tip to favor the predator, while environmental or genetic disadvantages—weather, starvation, disease, or deformity—weigh in against prey. The proverbial blood lust of the fox in the henhouse may be nothing but a projection of human proclivities, an assignment of irrationality to creatures that cannot object. Evolutionary progress, the fine-tuning of survival, instead seems to drive animal surplus killing. In a land of feast and famine it makes sense for bears, as it does for people, to stockpile whenever they can. Though they may take the occasional caribou calf, barren-ground grizzlies scrape the barrel's bottom while their southern cousins fatten up on salmon. (Musk oxen *do* thrive in places where bears are absent or find abundant and diverse food.) More importantly, nature urges all beings to realize their full potential. Surplus killing refines instincts. It polishes reflexes. It calibrates skills. Much pleasure springs from physical mastery, from the deft pitting of bodies against each other and of wits against world—any athlete, hunter, wild child, or animal intuits this.

Evolution never tires of new designs. Congruent with science, many Eskimo elders believe that wolves created caribou and vice versa. The same selective pressure keeps working on musk oxen and bears: in the keen presence of each other, both become faster, stronger, smarter, more alert and enduring, or else drop from the race. Species are not fixed, yet rarely do we get to witness their changing. At times, gene flows stagnate before drying up; at other times, they merge, gain momentum, and animate bastard forms. A recent Arctic example comes in the form of hybrid bears.

Last spring, a trophy hunter accompanied by a guide killed an animal on Banks Island, Canada, that resembled a polar bear with soiled fur and sooty rings around the eyes. Closer inspection also revealed long brown claws, a dish-shaped snout, and a humped back—all typical grizzly bear features. At seven and one-half feet, this bear was much shorter than the average polar bear but showed the small head suited to hunting seals through holes in the ice. DNA tests confirmed the unique animal to be the offspring of a polar bear sow and a grizzly boar. While both species have produced fertile cubs in zoos, crossbreeding has never before been documented in wild populations.

According to biologists, polar bears branched off from grizzlies that ventured onto the frozen ocean to stalk marine mammals. Shrinking sea ice may now force polar bears to adopt landlubber ways; platinum-blond seal hunters are reconnecting with their bruin cousins, which in turn travel farther north and can be seen feasting on whale carcasses in polar bear company.[9]

What should we call such crossovers? Grolar bears? Pizzlies? How will we pigeonhole a rapidly shifting world? The dilemma runs deeper, though, than mere problems with taxonomy.

Like hybrid bears, the last musk ox topples notions of ecosystem stability, a cornerstone of theories that satisfy our cravings for harmony, permanence, and smooth functionality. It compels us to accept extinction, to refrain from fixing what is not broken, but also to ask ourselves if our hands truly are clean. It raises questions that cut close to the bone. Can we embrace Nature unruly, Nature in flux? Is human-caused local extinction, the muting of voices in a landscape's register, less lamentable than its global counterpart? And ultimately: do we dare reassess our responses to environmental threats, or are we bull-headed enough to repeat destructive behavior, hastening our own end?

Outlining a philosophy of sound land management, Aldo Leopold cautioned us to preserve every cog and wheel—and by implication complete workshops—when tinkering. The realization that we don't even hold all the blueprints or fully grasp the interlocking of parts can be as humbling as a face-to-face encounter with ice-age beasts.

Notes

[1] Frozen overflow that encases a stretch of riverbed even in late summer.

[2] In 2008, polar bears were listed as threatened in the United States and are now protected under the Endangered Species Act—the first listing ever as a result of global warming. Pro-development politicians vowed to contest the decision, and it remains to be seen if protective measures on a national *and* worldwide level will be implemented and if so, how effective they are.

[3] Long portrayed as solitary—if not downright antisocial, except for mothers with young kits—both sexes of these hunter-scavengers were revealed to be attentive parents. Although young wolverines are weaned and begin to leave their mother's side at six months, we found them still traveling with at least one parent and then—for another year, most often and most surprisingly—with their fathers.

[4] Populations of some northern species fluctuate slightly out of sync with each other. A proliferation of prey allows more predators to survive and procreate. When prey populations crash, due to disease, predation, or environmental factors, predator populations follow suit. The hare-lynx cycle is a classic example of this delicate dance of species.

[5] Grizzlies keep feeding on or return to kills and become defensive when surprised there.

[6] Mountain goats look like albinos only after they shed their old ivory winter coat. A winter skin could indeed be confused with that of a black bear subspecies whose pelage is honey-blond: British Columbia's Kermode bear. Southeast Alaska's glacier or "blue" bear, on the other hand, is colored slate gray. (We thus have a case of twice-mistaken identity here.)

[7] Reid, one of Canada's great artists, rendered this Raven story in a spectacular yellow-cedar sculpture housed at the University of British Columbia Museum of Anthropology.

[8] A beached paddle wheeler and historic site on the outskirts of Whitehorse.

[9] In the spring of 2008, Native hunters killed a polar bear near Fort Yukon, two hundred and fifty miles south of the Beaufort Sea. It was the longest recorded inland journey by an Alaska polar bear. Normally at that time of year, the animals would be foraging on the sea ice.

Contributors

Alaska's wildlife and landscapes have inspired **Nancy Behnken**'s art since she moved to Sitka in 1981. Working as a commercial fisherman allows her to pursue her artistic interests—which include wood engraving and illustration—during the winter. Her pen-and-ink illustrations have appeared in *Arctic Refuge: A Circle of Testimony* and several other books.

Mary Burns is the author of four books of fiction and numerous radio plays, including the series *A Yukon Quintette* for CBC, a nonfiction book, and two stage plays. Chair of Creative Writing at Douglas College for twelve years, she recently returned to full-time writing. She lives near Gibsons, British Columbia.

Douglas H. Chadwick, a Montana-based wildlife biologist, has written hundreds of articles and ten books on natural history and conservation. He is also a founding board member of Vital Ground, a nonprofit land trust that protects habitat for the grizzly bear and, by extension, for many other species.

Craig Childs—naturalist, adventurer, and frequent contributor to National Public Radio's *Morning Edition*—lives with his wife and their two sons at the foot of the West Elk Mountains in Colorado. His highly acclaimed books include *The Secret Knowledge of Water, Soul of Nowhere, The Way Out,* and *House of Rain*.

James Michael Dorsey is an author, photographer, and explorer in search of stories and adventure. He is also a certified marine naturalist and sea kayaker. When not living with indigenous tribes to record their cultures, he travels the Rim of Fire in search of whales.

Lynn DeFilippo is a teacher, spinner, and outdoors enthusiast living in Cantwell. A transplant from the East Coast, she has lived in Alaska for eleven years. When she's not crafting qiviut, or teaching school, she can be found out in the country. This is her first published work.

Michael Engelhard has authored and edited several books of nature writing, including *Redrock Almanac* and *Where the Rain Children Sleep*. A cultural anthropologist by training, he migrates between the Colorado Plateau and Alaska, where he works as a wilderness guide. His fascination with wildlife attests to the incorruptibly feral side of *Homo sapiens*.

Maria Finn's travels in Latin America resulted in two anthologies— *Cuba in Mind* and *Mexico in Mind*—and a nonfiction study-abroad course, which she designed and taught. She has written for numerous travel magazines and currently teaches English in Brooklyn Heights. Her forthcoming memoir describes how she learned to tango.

Poet **Erling Friis-Baastad** was born in Norway, raised in Virginia, and has spent most of his adult life in Canada's Yukon Territory. His most recent book is *Wood Spoken: New and Selected Poems* (Northbound Press/Harbour Publishing). He is an editor with the *Yukon News* in Whitehorse.

Daniel Glick is the Colorado-based author of *Monkey Dancing: A Father, Two Kids, and a Journey to the Ends of the Earth*. He is also a contributing author to the photo book *The Last Polar Bear*. A former *Newsweek* correspondent, his writing has appeared in a dozen national magazines.

Jo Going's book of poems and paintings, *Wild Cranes* (National Museum of Women in the Arts), won the Library Fellows Award. She lives in Homer, Alaska, where everybody is either an artist or fisherman. Her writing also appeared in the *New Art Review*, *Driftwood*, *Crosscurrents*, *Bloomsbury Review*, and other journals.

Jennifer Hahn's award-winning *Spirited Waters* is an account of soloing the Inside Passage in a kayak. Hahn studied under Pulitzer Prize–winning author Annie Dillard and lives in Bellingham, Washington, with her potter husband and dog, Gracie. She is currently at work on a memoir and a book about harvesting wild plants.

Author, teacher, radio broadcaster, dramaturge, outdoor adventurer, and remote settler **Daniel Henry** lives with his psychotherapist wife and eleven-year-old son on the roadless side of a bay eight miles from Haines, Alaska, shared with gratitude with bald eagle, river otter, Sitka spruce, no-see-um, bear, moose, lichen, toad, vole, and crow.

Karsten Heuer is a wildlife biologist and park warden, who, for the past decade, has spent much of his time on foot and skis following some of North America's most endangered wildlife. He is the author of the award-winning *Being Caribou*, which chronicles a trek with the Porcupine Caribou Herd.

Marybeth Holleman's most recent book is *The Heart of the Sound*. Her work has appeared in publications including *North American Review*, *Orion*, *Christian Science Monitor*, *Alaska Quarterly Review*, *Sierra*, *American Nature Writing*, and *The Seacoast Reader*. A North Carolina transplant, she has lived in Alaska for more than twenty years.

Nick Jans is the author of eight Alaska books, including *The Grizzly Maze* and *The Last Light Breaking*. He has written hundreds of magazine articles, is a longtime contributing editor to *Alaska*, and a member of *USA Today*'s board of editorial contributors.

Kaylene Johnson is a longtime Alaskan who makes her home on a small farm outside Wasilla, Alaska. Her books include *Sarah*, *Portrait of the Alaska Railroad*, and *Trails Across Time*. Her award-winning essays and articles have appeared in *Alaska*, the *Los Angeles Times*, *Spirit*, and other publications.

Captain **Loretto Jones** works with the Alaska Marine Pilots, LLC, in Dutch Harbor. When not at sea, she teaches creative writing classes for the community of Unalaska. Loretto's experiences as a commercial fisherwoman and diver in Alaska are what her fiction, nonfiction, and poetry are about—life on the edge.

Steve Kahn is a lifelong Alaskan currently living on the north shore of Qizhjeh Vena (Lake Clark) in southwest Alaska. He is coauthor of *Lake Clark National Park and Preserve* (Alaska Geographic Association, 2008). His work has appeared in a number of publications, including *Alaska*, *ISLE*, and *Pilgrimage*.

Carol Kaynor is originally from Massachusetts but has lived in Fairbanks for thirty-one years, virtually her entire adult life. She has written about dog mushing and skijoring for *Mushing Magazine*, *Dog World*, and *Dog Sport Magazine*, among others, and has been published in *Ice Floe* and the *Alaska Quarterly Review*.

Hank Lentfer lives with his wife and daughter in Gustavus, Alaska, where he grows potatoes, watches cranes, and writes when the weather is crummy. He is the coeditor of *Arctic Refuge: A Circle of Testimony* and author of the forthcoming book *Faith of Cranes*.

Nancy Lord, based in Homer, Alaska, is the author of six books—three story collections and three works of creative nonfiction. She holds an MFA from Vermont College and teaches creative writing for the University of Alaska. She has received fellowships from the Alaska State Council on the Arts and the Rasmuson Foundation.

Christine Lowther is coeditor of *Writing the West Coast: In Love with Place* and author of *New Power* and *A Cabin in Clayoquot*. Her work has been featured on CBC Radio's *North by Northwest* and published in anthologies and periodicals including the *Vancouver Sun*, *The Fiddlehead*, and *The Beaver*.

Jo-Ann Mapson is the author of nine novels, most recently *The Bad Girl Creek* series and *The Owl & Moon Café*. She teaches summers at the University of Alaska Anchorage low-residency MFA in Writing program and lives with her husband and dogs in New Mexico, where she is at work on a new novel.

Debra McKinney is a longtime writer for the *Anchorage Daily News*. She and photographer Fran Durner won the national Dart Award, and she was also part of the team that won a Pulitzer Prize for the *People in Peril* series. McKinney and her husband spend summers at their cabin near Fairbanks.

Fairbanks writer **Debbie S. Miller** has explored and written about Alaska's wilderness and wildlife for the past three decades. Her book *Midnight Wilderness: Journeys in Alaska's National Wildlife Refuge* describes her many adventures there. Miller has authored numerous articles and essays—including one for *Arctic Wings*—and ten nature books for children.

Richard Nelson is a writer, activist, anthropologist, and subsistence hunter who lives in southeast Alaska. His books include *The Island Within* and *Heart and Blood*. He hosts his own radio show and frequently speaks on conservation issues. His ethnography *Make Prayers to the Raven* became an award-winning PBS television series.

Nita Nettleton grew up in Anchorage, raised by homestead dogs. The author of *The Wake-up Call of the Wild* has slung hash, weighed trucks, and worked in tourism as well as for the federal government. She now is exploring points south to see what the birds were talking about.

Drew Pogge is associate editor at *Backcountry Magazine*. His stories, essays, and poems have appeared in numerous publications, including *Backpacker, Powder, High Country News,* and *E—The Environmental Magazine*. He writes primarily about his skiing, climbing, biking, and hiking experiences, and lives in Colorado. He is a big fan of coyotes.

Ned Rozell is a contributing editor to *Alaska* and science writer for the University of Alaska's Geophysical Institute. In more than five hundred articles, he has popularized research for nonscientists. His book *Walking My Dog, Jane* chronicles an eight-hundred-mile hike along the trans-Alaska pipeline. He has lived in Fairbanks since 1986.

Carolyn Servid is the author of the essay collection *Of Landscape and Longing*. She edited the award-winning anthology *From the Island's Edge: A Sitka Reader,* and coedited *The Book of the Tongass* and *Arctic Refuge*. She contributed to *Home Ground: Language for an American Landscape,* edited by Barry Lopez, and lives in Sitka, Alaska.

Peggy Shumaker's memoir, *Just Breathe Normally,* grew from a severe car accident. *Blaze,* a collaboration with Alaska painter Kesler Woodward, is her newest book of poems. Professor Emerita at the University of Alaska Fairbanks, she teaches in the Rainier Writing Workshop. Her NEA Fellowship–winning work has been published internationally.

Ana Maria Spagna lives and writes in a remote community in the North Cascades accessible only by boat or float plane. Her first book, *Now Go Home: Wilderness, Belonging, and the Crosscut Saw,* was named a Best Book of 2004 by the *Seattle Times*.

Permissions

DATE DUE

~~MAR 1 0 2017~~